A PRESCRIPTION FOR HAPPINESS

*The Ten Commitments to
a Happier, Healthier Life*

DR MARK ROWE

First published in 2015 by
Dr Mark Rowe
Waterford Health Park, Waterford City, Ireland.

All rights © 2015 Dr Mark Rowe

Paperback	ISBN: 978-1-909483-81-1
Ebook – mobi format	ISBN: 978-1-909483-82-8
Ebook – ePub format	ISBN: 978-1-909483-83-5
CreateSpace	ISBN: 978-1-909483-84-2

All rights reserved. No part of this book may be reproduced or utilised in any form or by any means electronic or mechanical, including photocopying, filming, recording, video recording, photography, or by any information storage and retrieval system, nor shall by way of trade or otherwise be lent, resold or otherwise circulated in any form of binding or cover other than that in which it is published without prior permission in writing from the publisher.

The right of Dr Mark Rowe to be identified as the author of the work has been asserted by him in accordance with the Copyright, Designs and Patents Act 1988.

Produced by Kazoo Publishing Services
222 Beech Park, Lucan, Co. Dublin
www.kazoopublishing.com

Kazoo Publishing Services is not the publisher of this work. All rights and responsibilities pertaining to this work remain with Dr Mark Rowe.

Kazoo offers independent authors a full range of publishing services. For further details visit www.kazoopublishing.com

Cover design by Lee Grace
Printed in the EU

Table of Contents

Foreword — viii
Introduction *Seeing Things Differently* — xii

PART 1 *The Happiness Revolution*

Chapter 1	*What is Happiness?*	23
Chapter 2	*Seven Poison Dwarfs*	42
Chapter 3	*Seven Happy Dwarfs*	66
Chapter 4	*The Journal – Fine-tuning Your Psychological Fitness*	91

PART 2 *My Charter for Action*

Ten Commitments to Expand Your Happiness — 129

The First Commitment: *Gratitude – Dynamite for Your Well-being* — 131

The Second Commitment: *Kindness and Compassion – Live to Give* — 142

The Third Commitment: *Great Relationships – A Recipe for Real Contentment* — 153

The Fourth Commitment: *Goals That Allow You to Grow* — 167

The Fifth Commitment: *Making Time – For What Matters*	188
The Sixth Commitment: *Exercise – The Greatest Pill of All*	202
The Seventh Commitment: *Realistic Optimism – Oxygen for Opportunity*	221
The Eighth Commitment: *Simplicity – The Ultimate Sophistication*	232
The Ninth Commitment: *Spirituality – The Purpose of Life is a Life of Purpose*	241
The Tenth Commitment: *Courage – The Courage to Choose*	252
Afterword: *Discovering What Really Matters*	261
Acknowledgements	266
Further Reading	268
Reading Group/Book Club Guide	271

'If I were to wish for anything, I should not wish for wealth and power, but for the passionate sense of what can be, for the eye which, ever young and ardent, sees the possible. Pleasure disappoints, possibility never. And what wine is so sparkling, what rose so fragrant, what so intoxicating as possibility!'

SOREN KIERKEGAARD

Foreword

For the past twenty years my life has revolved around my work as a family doctor, or General Practitioner, in Waterford City, Ireland. I've diagnosed and treated people in consulting rooms at my practice, currently the Waterford Health Park, but also in their homes, work places, and even in dressing rooms at sports fixtures. I've been asked for – and happily given – advice in the supermarket, at the gym and in the car park. Irrespective of place or time, as far as I was concerned it was all part of what working as a doctor in your community meant.

The majority of my work has been in my consulting room; a quick 'back of the envelope' guesstimate of well over 40,000 hours and 160,000 direct doctor-patient consultations during that time. Of course telephone advice and paperwork add other layers – not to mention the bit of a chat when you're out and about.

Over that time, I have been privileged to meet so many inspirational people who have triumphed over adversity – and their courage continues to inspire me. In fact, it's been a real insight for me to appreciate, at first hand, the vital connection between body and mind, emotions and energy, happiness and holistic well-being. Unfortunately, and all too often, I have also witnessed another kind of connection; that between negative thought patterns, negative emotions and ill health. Through all of this – and by reflecting on my own experiences, both personally and professionally – I have come to realise that we really all do see the world, not as it is, but as we are.

Life can be just like a mirror; how you are on the outside is simply a reflection of who you are on the inside. Seneca, the Roman stoic philosopher who lived more than two thousand years ago, wrote that as long as you live, you should keep learning *how* to live; that the reality of your everyday experience is the best classroom to learn from. It is an opportunity to make real and ongoing improvements in your thinking and to expand your happiness; nothing is set in stone. For the gift of these insights I am deeply grateful, for all my experiences, personally and professionally; understanding that they have all contributed to the person I am today. Having the courage to not only accept what you can't change without judgement, but to improve what you can, is a choice for each and every one of us, opening up the possibility for even more happiness in this journey called life.

With the rise of consumerism, the culture of the 'pill for every ill' and increasingly the 'ill for every pill' has arrived. The quick fix and sticking plaster solutions are so often a measure of value from a system that encourages people to be passive consumers of healthcare – rather than active participants in their own health and well-being. Too often, this neither cultivates an appreciation of the root cause of many symptoms, nor promotes a unified understanding of life. And it rarely leads to healing and transformation.

Now don't get me wrong, I'm not suggesting throwing the baby out with the bath water. From life-saving chemotherapy to the power of bug-busting penicillin and the blood thinning properties of aspirin, modern medicine has an important role to play. Working as a doctor for twenty years I know this. Drugs can be an important player but they simply shouldn't be the stars of the show!

Modern doctors are grounded in science. They are trained in the causes and treatment of disease, backed up by an endless parade of facts and figures. But this can come at the expense of *caritas* and compassion, those very qualities that enrich and distinguish our humanity. The person behind the patient, the 'care' in the word healthcare, can, at times, be a mere afterthought to the juggernaut of test and treat, prescribe and promise. Of course, the art of good medical practice is to be able to marry the two, to combine the physical with the psychosocial, the science with the complex art of interpersonal human relationships.

Traditionally, Western medicine has a focus on science and technology; especially technology that impacts the outer world. In the East, the focus is more on the mind and how different states, including happiness, can be achieved. I believe in the possibility of a more holistic and finely balanced approach to health. An approach where East meets West in an integrated interdependent manner; where philosophy and wisdom merge with science and new understanding.

Doctors diagnose and treat, prescribe and promise, comfort and cure; they are the ultimate 'sorter-outers'. But behind the calm veneer of prescription pad and stethoscopes, the truth is that modern doctors have no magical powers or mysterious elixirs. The philosopher Cicero once said we should all be doctors to ourselves. And of course the only person any of us can change is ourselves. Physician, first heal thyself!

Doing the inner work that brings about such a change requires real courage, because knowing what to do and doing are poles apart! As the philosopher Plutarch wrote, what you achieve inwardly determines outer reality, opening your heart to the possibility of even more love and heartfelt joy, as well as hope and interest and inspiration and enthusiasm and fun. And appreciating that inner peace and contentment are the greatest prizes of all, so worth fighting for; a real prescription for happiness.

And so in sharing this journey of discovery, my hope is that – like me – you will develop new insights to support the possibility of transforming your thinking, improving your health and expanding your happiness.

Introduction

Seeing things differently

October 2009. With the global economy in the midst of the biggest downturn in living memory, Ireland, caught on the wrong side of the credit crunch, was in big trouble. With mass unemployment and negative equity affecting thousands of Irish families, the country was awash in a tsunami of fear, misery and negative stress. Through my daily work as a doctor, I was encountering so many harrowing stories. Stories of people losing their jobs, their homes, their futures; stories of families stretched to the limit, struggling to survive, searching desperately for meaning.

As I reflected on some of these experiences, I realised that, important though it was, simply alleviating suffering or medically treating and 'curing' depression wasn't going to be enough. Treating depression was not necessarily going to do anything to cultivate inner happiness and well-being. Treating anxiety was not going to teach the much-needed skills of realistic optimism. This was an 'Aha moment' for me as I realised why a different approach was needed for some of the people that I was trying to help and support. More than pills or Prozac, it was clear to me that they desperately needed – and were entitled to – new possibilities. And once you know your why, the how gets easier!

Several years ago, I went to Rome with my wife for a three-day break. One of the world's most captivating cities, at its heart is the stunningly beautiful and deeply inspiring Bramante-designed dome of St Peter's Basilica and the Sistine

Chapel. Along with its Michelangelo-painted ceiling, there is a stunning painting, *The Last Judgement*, on the back wall. A prolific Renaissance sculptor and artist, Michelangelo had the habit of signing his paintings in the bottom right-hand corner with the letters *alpha* and *omega*, the first and last letters of the Greek alphabet. In the beginning and in the end; begin with the end in mind – what a wonderful metaphor for goal setting! When once asked how he sculpted his masterpieces, Michelangelo apparently replied that he got the block of marble – and imagined the end sculpture. He would then chip away everything that was not part of the sculpture, just as we need to chip away at all those fears and limiting beliefs that can hold us back from revealing the masterpiece I believe is within us all.

Nearby on the walls of a room called the *Stanza della segnatura* are a series of frescoes. Commissioned by former Pope Julius II, the frescoes were painted by Raphael about the same time as Michelangelo was painting the ceiling of the Sistine Chapel. The last one, *The School of Athens*, particularly captured my attention. It is a wonderful painting, representing the greatest minds; a gathering of scientists, thinkers, mathematicians and philosophers through different time periods. In the centre of the painting are Plato and Aristotle, those two supreme philosophers each with their contrasting views on life. Plato is pointing up to the perfect world of forms in the heavens; his student Aristotle points downwards, reflecting that miracles are rooted in the clay, not the stars. And under his arm, Aristotle carries his book, *The Nicomachean Ethics*. Written over 2,300 years ago, this was a philosophical exploration of the good life, character and virtue; a bible of happiness and well-being.

So much wisdom represented in one painting. My eyes were opened in a new way to those timeless, transcendent truths of philosophy and to the exciting possibility of how they can integrate with health to support improvements in our lives. The philosopher Cicero once said that philosophy enables you to become capable of being a doctor to yourself so that you can live a healthier, happier and more fulfilled life. That message really resonated with me, this very old idea of people taking ownership and responsibility for their own health, happiness and well-being.

Philosophy promotes self-help in a broad, ethical way that supports our connection with our conscience, our community and with the cosmos. Socrates, the father of medicine, said that 'the unexamined life is not worth living'. By getting to know ourselves and our unconscious beliefs, we can change those beliefs and create new ways of thinking, feeling and behaving. These principles and ideas of ancient Greek philosophy are at the very heart of talking treatments and of therapies like cognitive behavioural therapy (CBT), an evidence-based approach to relearning emotional responses.

The topic of happiness and well-being has been studied for thousands of years as people have searched for and explored the keys to happiness. Confucius went from village to village preaching his message for fulfilment. Epicurus extolled the virtues of the pleasurable life, Seneca the stoical nature of things. Marcus Aurelius wrote about being the cliff against which the waves crash, but which stands firm. Reading more extensively about these wise philosophers, and integrating their time-tested principles into my own life and the lives of my patients, has become the bedrock for my new prescription for happiness.

Psychology as a profession has traditionally focused on human weakness, mental illness and various types of dysfunction; on what was *wrong* with people and on how their suffering could be relieved. Positive psychology is a new, exciting, evidence-based approach to well-being. Pioneered by the brilliant American psychologist, author and thought leader

Martin Seligman, it focuses on what is *right* with people, on *why* we are happy and on the essential question of 'what makes life worth living?' Positive psychology includes the study of positive emotions, human strengths and achieving more meaning and resilience in your life; qualities so desperately needed in today's world. Unsurprisingly, this science of happiness and flourishing has gone viral around the world as people have begun to embrace the possibilities for their own lives. Governments and policy makers are also getting in on the act with the tiny principality of Bhutan now using Gross National Happiness, GNH, instead of GDP, as a marker of the country's success. In 2012, the United Nations General Assembly declared 20 March as the International Day of Happiness in order to recognise the pursuit of happiness and well-being as fundamental universal goals.

When I had developed the Waterford Health Park in 2008, as a new model of community-based healthcare for my community, I was invited to join *Leading by Design*, a veritable Noah's Ark of leaders from radically different backgrounds. The architects, designers and thought leaders who comprise *Leading by Design* have in common a passionate commitment to improvements in health and healthcare, through a more effective and empathetic design of the environment. Here, I found myself spending time professionally with people who weren't medics; people who saw things very differently from me but with the same passion for improving health and healthcare. Learning from the experiences of others was challenging and energising and encouraged me to think differently. I began to imagine the possibility of redesigning health, through the eyes of a designer and using the backdrop of my own medical background. What would that look like? How might it be different from what exists already? How could this support new possibilities for the well-being of patients? In recent years, by learning to reflect on my experiences of what I do (as a medical doctor, educator and employer) as well as who I am as a person, I have come to *know* things very differently. Less emphasis on illness and more on wellness; less on treatment and more on prevention; less on healthcare and much more on happiness and health.

Several years ago, a local business owner asked me to speak to her staff as part of their annual wellness programme. By the time of her invitation, I had been speaking for many years to all sorts of groups on a variety of illness-related topics from depression to dementia, high cholesterol to heart disease – always with an emphasis on prevention and staying well. But my response to this invitation was different. I suggested a workshop on happiness and how important it was for the well-being of her people. To her credit, she was very enthusiastic and readily embraced the idea so that, on a wet rainy day in early November, about fifty of her staff became my first guinea pigs! A leap of faith on their part and on mine too, perhaps! How would this message about happiness be received? Was it something doctors should be talking about? I needn't have worried; the message was embraced with such enthusiasm and from the intensity of the engagement and the unsolicited positive feedback received in the days, weeks and months that followed, I knew I was on to something significant.

There was a real appetite for the message that health is about being all you can be; for an embrace of the connectivity between psychological fitness, emotional vitality, robust relationships and the golden egg of great physical health; for the idea that all of us have the power to change, improve – and choose to become happier. So I started to deliver health seminars and educational talks about happiness and health leadership to groups of people from diverse backgrounds; exploring, experimenting with different teaching modalities, taking feedback, reflecting, learning from my experiences, making improvements and – most importantly of all – having fun! And all the time seeing what I was doing as part of a bigger experiment in trying to figure out how to be a more effective resource to support people in improving their lives.

By integrating these timeless truths of ancient philosophy with the powerful purpose of positive psychology, I have developed a new understanding of 'health' and of the natural synergy between our physical health, psychological fitness, emotional vitality and the quality of our relationships. Having four strong elements promotes balance, allowing you to bounce back with purpose from life's challenges. This includes the passion and purpose with which we go about our daily activities; how we organise around our priorities and set and work towards goals consistent with our values. Not least, this new understanding reflects our sense of legacy; how we can be of most service to others while realising more of our unique potential.

And so I started to apply some of these techniques and messages in my work as a doctor. Encouraging people to keep a journal, and build awareness of how negative thoughts and emotions may be holding them back. Understanding the importance and power of expressing gratitude, by writing down three things each day they felt genuinely grateful for. Using the journal to monitor diet and exercise patterns, to build great habits, and to set and work towards goals, for the physical, emotional, psychological and relationship aspects of their health and well-being. Learning how to reflect on their experiences as an opportunity to gain valuable insights and support real improvements. Working on the ten commitments to expand and enhance their happiness. The results I observed were improved physical fitness, more focus on what's important, an expanded sense of happiness and contentment – in some cases, a complete transformation.

This wonderful journey of learning has given me a new lens of understanding through which the lives of those around me, as well as my own life, have come into much sharper focus. Of course, the existence of a strong connection between mind and body is no secret. Philosophers of old, like Plato, recognised this link thousands of years ago. I'm reminded of his words of wisdom that often the greatest mistake physicians can make is when they attempt to cure the body without attempting to cure the mind; that the mind and body are one and should not be treated separately, that the part can never be well unless the whole is well. Continuing to meet this challenge of how to improve 'health' in a way that supports my becoming a more effective resource for people to make meaningful improvements in their lives has become my most important professional goal.

The very question 'Am I happy?', in itself, can create the illusion that happiness is an all-or-nothing, zero-sum game; that you either are happy or you are not. This can foster discontent, dissatisfaction and a deep sense of frustration. Through my experiences, I have learned that a much better question might be 'How can I become happier?' Hence, the idea for this book. In the course of writing it, I have discovered that the answer to this question is a lifelong journey, not some fairy-tale destination of happily ever after. You can choose to become happier while being content right now; you can consider my ten commitments as your prescription for a happier, healthier life.

To become happier, I believe you need the wisdom to understand what's really important in life. In Part 1 of the book I have explored some key foundations to happiness, including an understanding of what happiness is – and some of the more interesting facts and fallacies surrounding it. The importance of how emotion impacts on your happiness and well-being is discussed in chapters that consider both negative and positive emotion (poison and happy dwarfs). Psychological fitness, and its impact on your happiness, is explored through the power of keeping a journal and ways to fine-tune your mind. Your thoughts and beliefs can have a fundamental impact on your moment-to-moment experience of happiness!

Part 2 of the book explores a number of important choices you can make to become happier; what I call the ten commitments to expanding your happiness. I'm not suggesting that you need all ten; there is no 'one size fits all' here and you may naturally find some easier to apply and more suited to your personality than others. The key is to try some of these and see which ones work best for you. Your own unique path to optimal happiness and well-being is just that – yours!

Part 1

The Happiness Revolution

Chapter 1
What is Happiness?

Happiness may be one of those things you feel you don't need to define – you know it when you feel it. But before looking at ways to expand your happiness, it's useful to have a crystal-clear understanding of what happiness is. And happiness can be a very hard term to pin down, define and accurately measure precisely because it can mean so many different things to different people. Perhaps happiness is the result of having someone to love, something useful to do and something to hope for.

There is clearly a difference between your moment-to-moment experience of happiness (which can vary from day to day depending on what's going on in your life at that particular moment) and your sense of reflected happiness, when you stop and ask yourself how happy you are with life overall. Martin Seligman, the pioneer of positive psychology, has broken happiness down to include pleasure, engagement and meaning. Daniel Kahneman, the Nobel prize-winning professor and author of *Thinking, Fast and Slow*, has described happiness as being a life rich in activities that are both pleasurable and meaningful. Aristotle, the Greek philosopher, described happiness as the chief good or '*summum bonum*', the meaning and purpose of life, the whole aim and end of human existence. He used the term *eudaimonia*, which translates to 'human flourishing' rather than happiness per se.

What we do know is that happiness is an emotional state or feeling of contentment, fulfilment and well-being which triggers positive emotion; encompassing pleasure, engagement and meaning. Happiness includes the moment-to-moment feelings of happiness triggered by pleasure and positive emotions, as well as how you describe your life when you reflect on your overall degree of happiness.

Pleasure is a profound psychological need. The distant brighter future can keep us going for only so long. All of us need present benefit and a certain amount of instant gratification. The carrot is normally so much better than the stick! Think of a wonderful meal, a party with friends. There are so many sources of temporary pleasure in life. For me, these include the aroma of freshly ground coffee, a few squares of really dark chocolate, walking in nature, sitting at a warm fire doing nothing in particular. But just as in the financial world where past performance is no guarantee of predicted future returns, so pleasure alone is no guarantee of sustainable happiness. Pleasure is fleeting and must, by definition, be temporary and transient. Otherwise your brain would adapt and turn pleasure into routine. Overindulgence can cause tolerance and addiction, creating false expectations and psychological boredom. In fact some forms of temporary pleasure can cause real unhappiness. Think of a drug-induced high, of drunkenness, of all forms of dependence. Transient pleasures are temporary and come and go as night follows day; wonderful in their own right in the moment but only a temporary fix. Even the philosopher Epicurus, who extolled the virtues of pleasure as 'the beginning and end of the blessed life', also wrote about the importance of moderation and guarding against excess which could lead to pain. All that glitters is not gold!

Can you remember the excitement of a major purchase, like a new car? Shut your eyes for a moment and think about the experience: all those gadgets, the aroma of fresh upholstery, the shininess of the exterior. Fast forward a few months and all that excitement and newness has worn off, the novelty eventually becoming the norm as the new car becomes just the car. Welcome to the hedonic treadmill, what psychologists describe as the tendency to continually adapt quickly to changing circumstances until you return to your happiness set point. It might sound complicated, but all it means is that material possessions and accomplishments on their own only temporarily raise happiness levels. So, if you're not careful, life can become a treadmill where you have to keep running faster and faster just to stand still.

The hedonic treadmill is one of the reasons why staying happy can be such a challenging journey. Modern media can bombard you with advertisements which subliminally promise more attractiveness or status or happiness from whatever they are selling. Much often wants more – ever-rising material expectations and demands have the potential to frustrate, dissatisfy and become genuine obstacles to real fulfilment. The more material possessions you seek, the more empty your life can become *unless* you also have the wisdom to appreciate that real and lasting happiness comes from within.

An interesting question to ask yourself is do your sources of temporary pleasure bring you happiness? Don't get me wrong, pleasure can be wonderful but on its own it is not enough. Sustainable happiness also requires a sense of engagement: being creative, energised and stretched to the limit, motivated for personal growth. William Butler Yeats, one of Ireland's best known poets, wrote that happiness is neither pleasure nor virtue, nor this nor that, but simply growth. We are happy when we are growing. And being passionate about what you do in life can bring so much happiness and freedom. Happiness can be the experience of the journey of climbing towards the top of a mountain that is of value to you, neither necessarily reaching the summit nor wandering aimlessly at the foothills.

Waterford City in Ireland was founded by the Vikings

in 914 AD. They had a saying that the North Wind made the Vikings and this can be true for you too. The ability to rapidly acclimatise to your circumstances can be enormously beneficial when it comes to helping you overcome adversity. It means a change for the worse in your material circumstances, or a major health challenge or disability issue won't necessarily affect your happiness over the longer term because you can adjust and adapt. This is good news! In fact, you have so much potential to overcome adversity, allowing you not only to bounce back but to bounce forward, building character, a sense of meaning and real accomplishment.

Nowadays, the long-term benefits of post-traumatic growth are often conveniently ignored, as meaning is often medicated away. This sense of purpose or meaning is also part of the package for sustainable happiness. A meaningful life requires that your goals are consistent with your values rather than the expectations of others. By taking personal responsibility and protecting your thinking, the human mind can become a meaning-making machine. Meaning can result from a sense of acceptance, achievement, fairness or intimacy, relationships, spirituality or connecting to your higher power. Carl Jung, the philosopher, wrote that the least of things with meaning is worth more in life than the greatest of things without it.

From an evolutionary viewpoint, this all makes sense. If some achievement or acquisition made you permanently happy, you would probably lose your motivation or initiative to learn new skills, to grow and progress. On the other hand, if loss or so-called failure led to a permanent sense of disillusionment, the net effects would be highly detrimental for your well-being and decrease your chances of survival.

Happiness – The Fairy Tale

Many lucky people, including me, have early childhood memories of being tucked in at night with a bedtime story.

A PRESCRIPTION FOR HAPPINESS

More often than not, it ended with some version of 'and the prince and the princess lived happily ever after'. This got me thinking about the notion of happily ever after; of happiness being some place you hope to get to when all your ducks are in a row. When you've got the prize, achieved promotion, or reached a destination of perfection that promises you eternal bliss. This fairy-tale notion of happiness is exactly that – a fairy tale, a false belief, a fantasy that a happy life equates to a flawless flow of positive emotions and stream of successes. It creates the false expectation that only one thing will make you happier, and carry you to the Valhalla of 'happily ever after'.

No wonder so many people get disillusioned with their imperfect lives. A full and fulfilling life inevitably contains setbacks, struggles, so-called failures for everyone. To feel and experience the full range of human emotions you need to give yourself permission to be human; to embrace defeats and those inevitable life disappointments while celebrating and appreciating your successes.

The bluebird represents hope and springtime renewal, and is a symbol of happiness in many cultures; this association may date back thousands of years. In Native American culture, the bluebird symbolises happiness, joy and contentment.

The Blue Bird, a play written by the Belgian playwright, Maurice Maeterlinck in the late nineteenth century and first published in 1907, is a masterpiece as a story about happiness. In this wonderfully crafted tale, two poor children, Mytyl and her brother Tyltyl, travel the world looking here, there and everywhere for the blue bird of happiness, only to arrive back home to discover that the blue bird had been there all along. Along the journey, they encounter the Land of Luxuries (a timely warning on materialism) – and happiness-producing experiences, such as *Seeing the Stars*

Rise, Innocent Thoughts and *Maternal Love*, all of which serve to reinforce Maeterlinck's message that true happiness lies in the simple things of life.

As Maeterlinck so wisely wrote: 'Each of us must seek out happiness for himself; and he has to take endless pains and undergo many a cruel disappointment before he learns to become happy by appreciating the perfect and simple pleasures that are always within easy reach of his mind and heart.'

Why Happiness?

It is a well-known fact that there is a tsunami of clinical depression in the Western world; that it will become one of the most common chronic illnesses by the year 2030. This fact is often relayed to me, by attendees at workshops and seminars, followed by the inevitable question; 'Is that why Mark, as a medical doctor, you spend so much time talking about happiness?'

Now the inexorable rise of depression and despair is indisputable; in fact depression rates have increased significantly since the 1950s. If we're to believe what we're told, it seems that almost everything is better now than in the 1950s (not just materially in terms of purchasing power and standards of living but with more employment, entertainment, and educational opportunities). Everything, that is, except human morale. Such is the prevalence and pervasiveness of low self-esteem, listlessness and lack of meaning in contemporary society, that this part of the twenty-first century could be called the Age of Melancholy. The truth is there are many people that are struggling through life, living far from their best.

Just think for a minute. How many people in your network do you know that are really thriving and living lives that are happy, purposeful and fulfilling? If it's more than 1 in 5, chances are you're lucky enough to be in the company of particularly

A PRESCRIPTION FOR HAPPINESS

positive people. According to Barbara Fredrickson, leading positive psychologist and author of *Positivity*, only about twenty percent of people are actually flourishing or living life at, or close to, their optimal potential, while the rest of us are plodding along in the middle somewhere or even worse languishing at the bottom.

But can you actually become happier? Good question! As a doctor, I would initially have thought 'Perhaps a little ...', while mostly believing that the attainment of happiness boils down to your personality and the part that lady luck plays in your life – in other words chance, circumstance and the cards you were dealt.

So it was a huge and unexpected surprise for me to discover from philosophy and positive psychology that you can *become* a lot happier! Furthermore you really should, because happiness is so good for your health and vitality. That's it; the reason why I am so interested in your happiness is that becoming happier can be a game changer for your health and sense of well-being! It's really that simple.

Now if you think about it, it kind of makes sense, but the idea of happiness being as important for your health as many of the old reliables like high blood pressure and raised cholesterol has, until recently, been a well-kept secret.

Ironically, during the 1665 Great Plague of London, being cheerful was one of the many ways believed to protect you from being afflicted! It wasn't true of course, but perhaps they were on to something. Because being happier really *is* good for your health. The first evidence to support this came from a study of people who lived very similar but simple lifestyles. Not an easy group to find but nuns, living together in religious congregations, fit the bill very well. Nuns from the School Sisters of Notre Dame had a tradition of requiring novitiates, on entering the nunnery, to write a short, handwritten autobiographical essay describing their hopes, ideas and views about their forthcoming vocation. Many years later these essays were analysed by psychologists (Danner, Snowdon and Freisen from the University of Kentucky), with every single written word coded for positivity or negativity. Some nuns expressed lots of positivity – such as love, contentment, gratefulness and their hopes for the future, while others wrote more negatively about suffering, guilt and repression.

When the psychologists looked at how long these nuns lived, they found the more positive nuns lived at least ten years longer than the more negative nuns. The degree of positivity expressed in the essays correlated closely with how long the nuns lived; in fact at any age the more negative nuns had twice the death rate of the more positive nuns.

All over the world, when asked what they want from life, people will offer up a number of different answers with friends and family as well as financial security among the most common responses. But ask people what they most want from life for themselves and their children and the most popular response is that they want happiness. Deep down people want to be happy. It generates that glow of contentment; you tend to gravitate towards it as you recall the glitter of the past and welcome new experiences with open arms.

The old paradigm was that happiness depended on what happened in your life. As you climbed the ladder of life success, eventually you could reflect and say: 'Now I can be happy!'

And while achievements and accomplishments in life can undoubtedly feel good, real success comes from being happier on the inside. This question of whether happiness leads to success was considered by a comprehensive review of over 200 studies involving more than 275,000 people by leading psychologists Lyubomirsky, King and Diener. In their fascinating article published in *Psychological Bulletin* in 2005, they confirm that whether you want to define success by the quality of your relationships, career goals, or your health, being happier makes more good things happen and leads to more success in every major life domain – at work or at home. Happier people are more motivated, more resilient and better able to deal with adversity. Happier people are more helpful, creative, charitable, self-confident, with better self-control and coping ability.

Happiness is contagious. Choosing to expand your happiness supports your leadership, not just in your own life but in your family, organisation and community. Dr Nicholas Christakis, who along with James Fowler is the author of *Connected: The Surprising Power of Our Social Networks and How They Shape Our Lives*, has shown that just like a virus, happiness spreads in social networks out to three degrees of separation – a win-win-win. What this means is that people you don't even know can benefit from your leadership in choosing to expand your happiness.

The Chinese philosopher Confucius wrote that 'It is better to light one small candle than to curse the darkness.' Just as the small flickering flame from a candle can light up an entire physical space, so a brief happiness booster such as laughter can transform, inspire and invigorate your state of mind.

Life is neither the candle nor the wick; it is the burning. Buddha wrote that thousands of candles can be lit from a single candle and the life of that candle will not be shortened. Happiness never decreases by being shared. In sharp contrast to the idea that if you're winning, I must be losing, Buddha's inspiring candle analogy suggests that happiness is a positive sum game whereby everyone can be better off.

So I asked myself: 'Given how important happiness is for health, and given that there are skills you can learn to become happier, shouldn't everyone get to hear about them?' Hence this book, which is my commitment to support you in enhancing the quality of your everyday experiences and in expanding your happiness.

Exploding the Myth

In order to better appreciate what happiness is, I believe it is useful to understand what happiness isn't! Here are some of the more prominent misconceptions about happiness today.

Happiness is self-centred, silly 'happyology'

This is an accusation often thrown at people who want to explore ways of becoming happier. Far from it: unhappy people tend to be the most introspective, self-absorbed and, more often, socially withdrawn. Happier people tend to be more forgiving, tolerant and patient than unhappy people. And why would you dismiss something that is so good for your physical health, psychological fitness and the quality of your relationships?

Happiness is about never being negative

No it isn't! Negative emotions – I call them the Seven Poison Dwarfs – have a role to play in the fullness of human experience. It's important to acknowledge and understand the role the poison dwarfs play in your life right now and to do the inner work that may be needed to put them back in their box. The key is to have the right ratio between your happy and poison dwarfs (positive and negative emotions). That ratio ought to be at least 3:1 – and that depends, to a large degree, on your own thinking!

Happiness is about luck and your life circumstances

The word 'happy' derives from the Icelandic word, *happ*, meaning luck or chance. And some people can be dealt a pretty lousy hand in life. But sustainable happiness is largely in your own hands; it's not about lady luck, losing weight or landing the jackpot.

Once your basic survival needs have been met, then only about ten per cent of your potential happiness is derived from your current life circumstances – a statistic that can shock, surprise and cause confusion. Many people pursue things in life because they believe they will make them happy. If you insist that happiness is determined by what happens to you in life, you will be left at the mercy of circumstances, with little control over your emotions. While you may be unable to change your circumstances, you *can* control your attitude and how you choose to see the world.

Happiness is a destination

This is the myth that once you have achieved a certain goal, landed your dream job, or made enough money, then you will be happy. In fact, simply wanting and chasing after things can create unhappiness. Just like the crock of gold under the rainbow, chasing after happiness can immediately put you at a distance from it, making it harder to achieve. Furthermore, once you get what you were looking for, your brain automatically starts looking for new benchmarks.

While working towards goals consistent with your values, your emotional well-being is enhanced. Happiness is taking the time to smell the roses today, while you are on the journey to the mountaintop. Don't let life pass you by awaiting perfection before you allow yourself to be happy. Stop waiting for future happiness; work on being happy today, right now, in this present moment.

Happiness is your entitlement

No it isn't! The pursuit of happiness may be enshrined in the American Constitution but it is still something you have to work on. A sense of entitlement is a sure-fire way to becoming unhappy. The explosion of the 'pill for every ill' culture has led to the presumption that Prozac or the like can make you happy; that happiness is as easy as popping a pill or shopping for the latest gadget or gizmo.

Now pleasure is easy and can make you feel better, boost your mood and it may well be worthwhile. But pleasure is different from happiness which also requires a sense of engagement and meaning – with these, in turn, requiring effort and thought. If you wanted to become physically fitter you wouldn't just decide to read a book about exercise; you'd have to work on it by building the habit of regular exercise. It's the same for your happiness: it's something you have to work on, part and parcel of your personal growth. The good news is that there is so much you can do to become happier, once you take control of your thoughts and emotions and start applying my ten commitments to expand your happiness.

Happiness comes from the toys you own!

Which of these things do you think would make you happier: an extra bedroom in your house, a new car, staying young or a better job? What would you think if I told you that the evidence suggests that NONE of these things will make you significantly happier? One of the great myths about happiness is that it is determined solely by how rich and materially successful you are, and how many 'toys' you have. In modern life success and happiness is often defined in material terms of power, prestige and possessions by a society that values wealth, numbers, and the measurable.

Over the past fifty years in the western world, despite incomes and living standards having improved, with more conveniences than ever available at the click of a button, happiness levels haven't significantly changed. Increasingly, many people struggle to achieve inner peace, real happiness or contentment.

A PRESCRIPTION FOR HAPPINESS

Happiness levels are set in stone

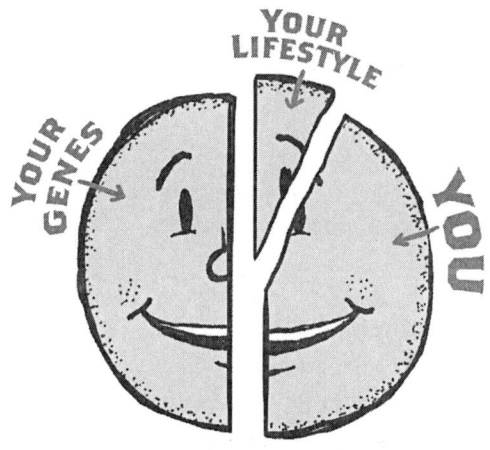

Far from it! In fact, only about fifty per cent of your potential happiness is inherited. Studies carried out on identical twins (same genetic make-up) have found that they share very similar levels of happiness, irrespective of whether they were raised together or separately. In terms of the nature-nurture debate, it is known that up to fifty per cent of your potential happiness comes from your genes (not your Levi 501s!). This means you have an inbuilt baseline happiness level or set point, which is the happiness level that feels most natural to you. And only about ten per cent of your potential happiness comes from your life circumstances.

The remaining 40 per cent is determined by your attitude and behaviour, the things you do or don't do, say or don't say, each and every day. The nuts and bolts of this '40 per cent solution' will be described later on in what I call the ten commitments to consider in order to expand your happiness.

A PRESCRIPTION FOR HAPPINESS

Happiness won't improve your performance

Yes it will! Being happier will boost your creativity, energy and performance, giving you a real edge in whatever way you want to define accomplishment or achievement, whether it's in sport, academics or the world of work.

Happiness is about eliminating weaknesses

No it isn't! Focusing on weaknesses gives voice to fear and trying to turn weaknesses into strengths will never happen. Some weaknesses – for example, the consequences of excess alcohol – can significantly affect your happiness and your health. As a depressant drug, alcohol can be a good servant but it is a very bad master and may need to be eliminated. But happiness is about identifying and using your strengths. And focusing on your strengths feels better, works better and quite simply is so much better for your happiness and well-being.

Happiness is only for the young and the healthy

Even though many people believe this one, nothing could be further from the truth. For many people, youth and younger years are often not the brightest in terms of your happiness. After a significant drop in happiness during your mid-forties (which coincides with the mid-life crisis) happiness levels tend to increase progressively up to your sixties, seventies or beyond. Probably the clarity of perspective when you're older allows you to value what's important and to live more in the present. Perhaps youth really *is* wasted on the young!

While becoming happier is really good for your health, it doesn't mean that developing illness or bad news is a permanent party pooper. Far from it! You have an incredible ability to develop post-traumatic growth, gain new perspective and bounce back with a renewed sense of meaning, transforming your happiness on a day-to-day basis. Being happier can improve mental health, build stronger immune systems and may well support better outcomes from chronic illnesses like heart disease and diabetes. A happier heart is a healthier heart!

Happiness can be bought

So, does more money make you happier? Yes it can – but then again it might not! Current understanding indicates that there is only a mild correlation between material wealth and long-term happiness, and this effect may be more temporary than you might think. In very poor countries where poverty threatens life itself, being richer does indeed predict greater happiness. In wealthier countries, there is a steady increase in well-being seen up to the point where people have the basics in life to survive. Once that tipping point is reached, further increases in material wealth do not necessarily lead to any greater sense of income-related happiness or well-being.

People tend to feel better when they feel they are above average and doing better than those around them. This law of comparison can be a powerful motivating tool for humanity. While comparing yourself unfavourably to others can lead to 'compareitis' – a major trigger of the poison dwarf called Envy – comparing yourself in a positive way to people less fortunate than you can trigger feelings of gratitude and happiness. The medieval Persian poet Saadi wrote eloquently in *The Rose Garden* in the year 1259: 'I bemoaned the fact I had no shoes, until I saw the man who had no feet!'

Money spent on others gives more happiness than money spent on you. Of course, material success can buy freedom from worry about the next pay check, liberate you from doing work that you don't find meaningful and allow you the time and space to follow your passions. That's a given! But expanding your happiness is far more likely if you spend money helping others (also known as 'prosocial spending') or on creating meaningful experiences with your family or friends. Elizabeth

A PRESCRIPTION FOR HAPPINESS

Dunn, co-author of *Happy Money: The Science of Smarter Spending,* describes how students, when given either $5 or $20 to spend, reported more happiness when spending the money on someone else rather than on themselves. Spending on others builds a more positive self-image as a kinder and more responsible person and strengthens relationships, all of which boost happiness.

Ever heard of the Midas touch and wondered where the term came from? Well, according to the philosopher Aristotle, King Midas is remembered in Greek mythology as a money-obsessed king who died of hunger because of his 'vain prayer' for the golden touch. Collecting more and more gold was his hobby, his joy and his life. As the story goes, he was counting his gold one day under a tree when he saw an old man asleep. This man was Sibelius from the court of Dionysus, the God of Wine. Midas took the old man into his house and looked after him for ten days. Dionysus subsequently thanked Midas by granting him a wish and warning him about his greed. Midas assumed that once he became immensely rich, his happiness would be assured forever. As a result, his wish was that everything he touched would turn into gold. Midas now believed that nothing could stop him from becoming the richest and happiest man in the world. So he touched his trees, the walls of the palace, his children – and everything turned to gold. However, Midas soon came to regret the short-sighted nature of his so-called bargain, as the food and wine in his mouth turned to gold before he could swallow them, and he died surrounded by golden plates and golden cups.

The message of this myth continues to ring true today, as people continue to search and strive for external sources of happiness and well-being. There are clearly some poor people who are very happy and some rich people who are miserable. Oscar Wilde, the nineteenth-century Irish writer, put it so clearly when he described the cheap cynics who constantly confuse price with value; they think happiness is money, and that personal worth is equal to net worth. Nothing could be further from the truth. Money and material success can be a real blessing in your life and even better when they allow you to help others. Now, don't misunderstand me, there's nothing wrong with wearing nice clothes, driving a nice car or living in a nice house – just don't expect those things on their own to make you permanently happy!

Happiness is not conducive with leading a moral life

Yes it is – because happiness is about meaning and purpose as well as about pleasure. There is an inbuilt morality in happiness and an inbuilt happiness in morality; they go hand in hand. This may go at least some way to explaining why religious belief (irrespective of specific type) is associated with higher levels of happiness.

Happiness is a one-size-fits-all prescription

There are many different ways that you can become happier, whether it's learning to be more present, bringing more positive emotion into your life or applying some of my ten commitments to expand your happiness. I'm not suggesting that all ten commitments will work equally well for you. There's going to be a certain amount of trial and error. What works best for you may be different from someone else; your unique prescription for happiness is YOURS!

Expanding your happiness; a choice YOU can make

Happiness is a skillset that can be learned, developed and improved over time. The fountain of happiness can be found in what you think or don't think, feel or don't feel and in what you do or don't do each and every day of your life. The key to your long-term happiness lies not in changing your genetic make-up (which is impossible), not in significantly changing your circumstances, such as seeking wealth or attractiveness or better friends, which is usually impractical, but, instead, in your daily intentional activities.

You have a choice in life: to count your blessings or to blame and complain; to strive for mastery or mediocrity; to hold on to your dreams or let them drown in a sea of negativity. The results you are producing in your life right now are largely a reflection of your current thoughts, emotions and actions. The good news is that if you choose to focus on the positive, on what's right with your life and your relationships, you will become aware of even more good things to focus on. By thinking more positive thoughts, you are able to cultivate more of the happy dwarfs (positive emotions). Appreciate the need for balance: psychological fitness, emotional vitality, strong relationships and the golden egg of great physical health. Begin with the end in mind; becoming happier is not only possible, it's your choice. And if you're interested in your health or that of your family or organisation, then expanding your happiness is also your responsibility.

Martin Seligman, the founder of positive psychology, has found that humans seem happiest when they have pleasure and engagement, relationships, meaning and accomplishments in their lives. Long-term sustainable happiness and well-being come from within. Choosing to expand your happiness is an ongoing commitment: a fundamental decision to become more aware of the potential for everyday happiness that lies inside you.

In this book I will show, firstly, why new awareness and understanding is needed about the power of negative emotions: what I call the Seven Poison Dwarfs! Just as passive smoking is a health hazard, carcinogenic and now rightly banned from most public spaces, so too can excess negative emotion have a similarly negative impact on your physical health, relationships and happiness. This is why you need lots of the happy dwarfs (positive emotions) to counteract them and flourish (in fact at least three happy dwarfs for each poison dwarf). Happiness is the crock of gold within; when you allow the rainbow of positive emotions (those happy dwarfs) to have a free rein in your heart and mind. Bringing more of the Happy Dwarfs into your life – Love, Joy, Hope, Inspiration, Enthusiasm, Interest, Fun; while keeping those Poison Dwarfs – Fear, Envy, Anger, Anxiety, Guilt, Shame, Sadness in their place is so important for your happiness and well-being!

Learn about the power of psychological fitness: how what you think and believe influences your happiness, and who you become. How many people set New Year resolutions to get healthier, and so join a gym, only to give up after a few weeks because they haven't addressed how they think and feel about themselves and their goals? One of the biggest obstacles to your own long-term happiness and improved health can be you! The quality of your own thinking and beliefs really do matter in encouraging and motivating you, from what you may need to do (become happier and healthier), to how to do it on a sustainable basis.

Ultimately, expanding your happiness is your choice; it's all about what you do, and what you do regularly matters so much more than what you do once in a while. The smallest of actions always exceeds the noblest of intentions. While knowledge is power, the application of knowledge over time can lead to true wisdom. The goal of this book is to refresh, renew and restate some of these timeless truths to support your choice to become happier and more contented. Expanding your happiness will give you more balance, harmony and fulfilment; a platform for success and a life of real significance. You can achieve more of your unique potential, become happier and healthier! To me it really now has become self-evident. And I hope it does for you too!

Chapter 2
Seven Poison Dwarfs

Smoke Signals for Change

After several years of working hard in other places, a colleague and I had started our own GP practice on 1 March 1999. Giving up the security of the regular pay cheque and taking the plunge into the unknown wasn't easy but it was the right thing to do in the circumstances. We managed to rent a space upstairs over a shop in my home city, right across the road from where I had grown up and where my parents still lived. Very local, very personal; so many vivid memories. We worked really hard getting the new business up and going and I must say I had such a sense of pride in what we achieved. We had furniture from home, nice prints on the walls, plenty of (up to date) magazines in the spacious waiting area, even a leather couch. We worked hard, the practice grew and everything was going well. Happy days!

Until almost a year later, the day everything changed. The unforgettable knock on my front door early that Friday morning early, waking me from my slumber. Aggressive, impatient, hurried. I rushed downstairs in my pyjamas. You'd better come quickly, Doctor, your practice is on fire.' On fire! Time seemed to stand still as I quickly dressed and rushed over to the practice. Neighbours with morning newspapers under their arms stood casually watching the billowing smoke, the searing flames. And as I watched the fire brigade doing their stuff, I had an overwhelming feeling that everything we worked so hard for was going up in smoke before my eyes. I felt numb.

A few hours later we were permitted to go in to see what remained of our workplace. I will never forget the smell, an all-pervasive pungent mixture of charred wood, smoke and fumes. And what looked like a burst red party balloon on the wall of the upstairs hall. Some party! What was that doing there? Getting closer, I realised this was no party balloon but what remained of our fire extinguisher!

We dusted ourselves down and worked through the weekend, fitting out a vacant property nearby. With all hands on deck, we were back open to serve our community the following Monday morning. But I wasn't back in business. Not really. You see I took that fire personally, and I was consumed by it. Behind the veneer of calm acceptance all those Seven Poison Dwarfs came to visit me, regularly. I felt angry – Why would someone do something like this to me in my own community? I felt anxious and fearful (CCTV footage had captured two hooded youths entering the premises with rucksacks; several separate fires had been set). Was this fire deliberate sabotage, arson or just random crime? There was never any convincing or credible evidence that it was deliberate or personal to me but I took it personally. Was there a possibility that they would come to my home next? I felt envious of colleagues working elsewhere in Ireland who, at that moment, had it so easy compared to me. I felt guilty that I hadn't foreseen this event as a possibility and taken additional security precautions. I also felt guilty for feeling guilty because thankfully no one had been hurt and I know only too well from my work about the real challenges people face day in and day out. Paradoxically I felt a sense of shame (because this wouldn't happen to anybody unless they deserved it, right?). Of course I felt sad. So the cumulative effect of these Seven Poison Dwarfs was that I ended up wallowing in my negativity. I went on a downward spiral for weeks afterwards, filled with negative thinking patterns including poor-me thinking, black-cloud thinking, making-assumptions thinking. Of course this fire was just a random arson attack but as Epictetus, the philosopher, wisely wrote 'People are not disturbed by things, but by the views they take of them.'

One day I woke up and realised I had a choice. I could continue to feel sorry for myself and wallow in my negativity but it wasn't going to bring the pre-fire situation back. Instead I could choose to let go of it, to accept that what had happened had happened and move on. Learning this power to choose, this path of self-acceptance, was a real gift for me. Thankfully nobody had died or had been injured in the fire, which had been contained before it had a chance to spread to adjoining premises. In fact there was so much about it to be grateful for. Things could have been so much worse. Now, more than fourteen years later, I look back on that fire with a deep and genuine sense of heartfelt gratitude. I am truly so grateful for that experience. In fact it was one of my most important experiences in terms of my own personal and professional growth. I can't imagine what my life would be like without it. Why? Because it has taught me the really valuable lesson of acceptance, shown me how resilient I am (how resilient we all are) and that ultimately in life it is not what happens to you but how you respond. That no matter how many times you get knocked back, what defines you is coming back again and again. I'm reminded often of the quote by Viktor Frankl 'That which brings light must endure burning.'

A PRESCRIPTION FOR HAPPINESS

We all face fires in our lives, adversity of one form or another, setbacks, disappointment. But there is always the spark of possibility for renewal, the sound of another door opening even as the noise of the one slamming shut in your face resonates loudly in your eardrums.

Can you think of previous 'fires' in your own life? And the opportunity to grow that has come from them?

Emotions allow you to feel what you are thinking at any particular moment; to determine what you pay attention to and how you make decisions. They influence how you judge risk, what you remember and the significance you put on life events. Emotions are nature's way of equipping you for survival; your gut instinct or primitive impulse to act – the automatic default you have for handling life's situations. There are two types of emotion: negative emotion and positive emotion. That's all well known. But what has been really interesting is appreciating how positive and negative emotion, more specifically the balance between them, can have such an impact on your overall happiness, health and well-being.

As the heartbeat of your thoughts, negative emotion is a hardwired survival tool. Thousands of years ago, this priceless skill helped to keep the caveman safe in a world full of danger and threats. And despite all the outward changes in the modern world, on the inside things are pretty much the same. Human beings instinctively take more notice of the negative than the positive in life, tending to remember rejection, frustration, and so-called failure much more clearly than success.

What about you? Think of something good that happened in your life recently. Now think of something not so good. Which do you recall more vividly? Chances are it's something negative. From my experience as a doctor, given the choice of hearing bad or good news, most people ask to hear the bad news first because it is considered more important. If you are like most people, you will tend to recall negative events much more readily than positive events, and spend more time and energy trying to figure out why something bad happened and what it means. Psychologists have figured out that you generally pay more attention to negative facial expressions than to pleasant ones; you are more motivated by avoiding loss than by possible gain.

Imagine that it is a beautiful summer's day and you are out for a walk in a woodland area filled with fragrant flowers and shrubs. With a warm sun at your back and an ever so gentle breeze, you feel so relaxed, connecting with nature, without a care in the world. Suddenly, a big brown bear jumps out from behind a tree, right into your path. You stop for a split second, shocked, startled and surprised. Will I hide behind those trees or run for my life?

So what happens? The emotional alarm centre in the brain, called the amygdala, goes off and all hell breaks loose! Rapid release of stress hormones, like adrenaline, flood your system, readying you for high alert, fight or flight. Within milliseconds, you will experience an intense sense of fear which shows on your face. Your heart rate skyrockets, your blood pressure shoots up and breathing slows down. Your blood shunts downwards into the muscles of your legs and is diverted away from the face, causing the face to go pale ('the blood runs cold'). You may freeze for a split second to decide what is going on and how to best react (whether it is safer to hide rather than to fight or flee). This classical fight or flight response will help you to run for your life away from that bear, unless you are feeling particularly brave or foolhardy and fancy your chances at taking him on!

This is the benefit of negative emotion, allowing you to take quick action; it is hardwired into your brain for good reason, to allow you to survive! Imagine if you did not have negative emotion. Fear and anxiety can help you to escape from dangerous situations and to learn to avoid those situations in the future. Without fear you might just sit down on the grass and simply wonder what the approaching bear was doing in the woods! Without anxiety, you might not be around tomorrow to tell your friends about that experience with the bear.

This hardwired emotional response in your brain is quite separate from your thinking brain, and has kicked in, before you have even had time to analyse what that bear was doing in the woods, the 'why me', 'why now' etc. These factors do not even come into it.

Once a strong negative emotion is turned on, the sophisticated thinking brain has difficulty in turning it off even if the thinking brain 'knows' that the threat from the bear is no longer there. Your emotions can literally have a mind of their own, and can hold views quite separate from those of a rational mind.

Getting back to the bear story, when you arrive home you may well be anxious, shuddering with fear as you relate your life-threatening experience to your family and friends. You may not sleep well that night and this hangover effect of stress may persist for days after your experience. If you are like most people, you are unlikely to go for a walk in those woods again. You might even end up getting post-traumatic bear syndrome!

To a large degree this depends on your mind sight. Do you remain focused on what has happened or can you see the silver lining? Are you grateful that you escaped the clutches of the bear? People who experience sudden shocks to the system, as in victims of severe road traffic accidents, fires and acts of terror or war, may have recurrent nightmares, sleep disturbance and chronic anxiety and may develop post-traumatic stress disorder. The good news is that people can be incredibly resilient and, despite – or perhaps because of – significant adversity, can bounce back and experience what's called post-traumatic growth and develop new perspectives and meaning.

Reacting to real or perceived threats is a real double-edged sword: on the one hand potentially life-saving, on the other an unnecessary and potentially health-damaging source of stress. The word 'perceive' is important here. Most negative emotion is not triggered by big brown bears but comes from negative thoughts which originate within you. Remember, you see the world not as it is, but as you are. Milton, the seventeenth-century poet, put it well when he wrote that the mind is its own place and can make a heaven of hell or a hell of heaven.

Negative emotion can be seen as the psychological equivalent of pain, a sign that your mental health is struggling just like physical pain is a sign that your body is suffering. But while you can pop a couple of painkillers for your sore back or creaky knee, it's not so easy to turn off negative emotion. Negative emotion tends to get the focus of your attention, narrow your range of thinking, and become even more prominent in your mind. It can pervade your perceptions, perspective and personality. In fact your perspective can become so skewed by the black cloud of negativity that you damage your ability to deal constructively with stress. As a result, you can become defensive in your decision-making and develop negativity bias; you become dejected, dispirited and disillusioned. Negative emotion is also highly contagious and can cause a lot of collateral damage. Holding on to negative emotion is like wearing an emotional straitjacket, restricting your emotional vitality and potential happiness.

The Seven Poison Dwarfs

Wanting to explore how emotion impacts the way we behave gave me the idea of the Seven Poison Dwarfs, a non-threatening way of labelling a negative emotion that is clearly separate from the person themselves. Perhaps this was a throwback to my own childhood years, recalling the original Snow White and the Seven Dwarfs, especially Doc and

Grumpy. The most important negative emotions are known by me as the Seven Poison Dwarfs because they have the ability to be so corrosive to your well-being. Toxic, raw and destructive they can cloud your thinking, cause confusion and poison your creative potential and happiness. And they can be so bad for your physical health. In fact you could say that more people die because of what's eating them up than from what they eat. Let's have a closer look at these Seven Poison Dwarfs and what they can do to you.

Fear

I call fear the supreme negative emotion, the biggest dwarf in the room, the king of the poison dwarfs. When you feel fear you can protect yourself from harm which may be mission critical for your survival (remember the big brown bear story).

But there are so many different types of misplaced fear that you may experience. Fear of criticism, conflict or compromise; fear of being different, growing old or making a fool of yourself; fear of being rejected, ridiculed or laughed at; fear of being judged, of disapproval, of being wrong; fear of what other people may think or do or say; fear of success or failure; fear of being poor, being hurt (emotionally or physically); fear of loss (of your life savings, sex drive, relationships, career, status in society) or letting go; fear of illness; fear of showing your own vulnerability; fear of the unknown, of scarcity (not having enough, not being enough), of change or new ideas; of love, of death, fear of life and living; fear of happiness; fear of fear itself. Fear, endless fear! Getting out of your comfort zone and making changes in your life can be really scary and all of these misplaced fears can keep you stuck. The expression 'frozen with fear' highlights the impact fear can have, causing you to avoid risk or spontaneity, to retreat, and to try not to.

Intense fear out of proportion to danger is known as a phobia. Common phobias affect about five to ten per cent of the population and include agoraphobia (fear of open spaces), social phobia (fear of humiliation and embarrassment while being observed by others), and nosophobia (fear of a specific illness like cancer).

A common fear seen in healthcare is fear of needles or doctors (especially ones wearing white coats!) leading to 'doctor avoidance' syndrome. But there is always a price to be paid when you don't face your fears, and in the case of 'doctor avoidance', the price may be your greatest asset (your health). For doctors, fear of litigation is one of the main drivers of 'defensive medicine', the explosion of – sometimes unnecessary – investigations in modern healthcare.

Fear of Criticism

Aristotle wrote that criticism is something you can avoid easily – by saying nothing, doing nothing and being nothing! Do you allow criticism to flatten, frustrate or deflate you, to hold you back in life, or do you use it as a motivational tool to improve? Do you do the best you can, regardless of who the so-called judges are?

Many people, as young children, had big dreams of becoming footballers, firemen or famous ballerinas. Big dreams can be as fragile as big balloons – and just as easily popped by the litany of negative messages, whether from your friends, teachers or parents. Don't do this, don't do that; stop doing this, stop doing that. You can't do this, you can't do that. Of course, sometimes negative feedback is critically important for your well-being and very survival as young children. But if there is not enough positive emotion in the game, then these negative messages can become deeply ingrained in your brain's computer. You may then spend the rest of your life selling yourself short, going along with the crowd, without stopping to question the validity of your beliefs and your thinking. Somewhere along the way you may become discouraged and disillusioned and those dreams may get quashed or forgotten.

Have you any dreams or goals you've let go of that you might want to rekindle?

Fear of Disapproval

I once remember hearing a wise man say that what anyone else thinks or says about you is none of your business. So true! In fact, being overly concerned about other people's opinions of you is like wearing a stiff emotional straitjacket – it's going to keep you stuck. But you know what? If you are going to wait until you have got everyone's approval you will never do anything. Think of Christopher Columbus who discovered America in 1492. At that time, the conventional wisdom was that the world was flat and one should never sail out of sight of the safety of the shore. However, he had the courage and the vision to sail out perpendicular to the shoreline and didn't let fear of disapproval, criticism or so-called failure stop him or slow him down. By leaving the safety and security of the known and venturing into the unknown, his reward was that he discovered America. Ultimately, all significant progress in the world depends on those people prepared to do just that; to take risks and follow their heart and conscience towards their dreams and goals.

Maybe there is something in your life that you've been keeping on hold, pending approval from someone else?

Fear of Failure

How do you deal with struggles, setbacks or so-called failures? Do you allow them to knock you down or do you get back up again? Do they give you the insight to focus on what is important for you? Do you use these experiences as an opportunity to grow?

Fear of failure is often driven by an all-or-nothing, win-lose, must-do thinking pattern; a rigid mind sight where a perfect outcome is the only show in town. Of course failure is simply feedback on performance. Someone says something or something happens, or someone doesn't say something and something doesn't happen. Often it is your interpretation of these events that creates the sense of failure or of success in your mind. And yet so many people don't ever change because getting out of your comfort zone can be so frightening, challenging and confusing. As a result, many people decide to just stay put and complain instead.

One of the best cures for fear of failure is exactly that – failure. Because just as the darkest hour comes before the dawn, so actual failure is almost never as bad as the dreaded fear of failing.

J.K. Rowling, the prolific author, in her Harvard commencement speech in 2008 spoke about the real value of so-called failure.

'Failure meant a stripping away of the essential. I was set free, because my greatest fear had already been realised, and I was still alive ... And so rock bottom became the solid foundation on which I rebuilt my life. Failure gave me an inner security that I had never attained by passing examinations. Failure taught me things about myself that I could have learned no other way. I discovered that I had a strong will, and more discipline than I had suspected; I also found out that I have friends whose value was truly above rubies ... The knowledge that you have emerged wiser and stronger from setbacks means that you are, ever after, secure in your ability to survive. You will never truly know yourself, or the strength of your relationships, until both have been tested by adversity.'

A PRESCRIPTION FOR HAPPINESS

Fear is a poison dwarf that I have known all my life. When I look back, sometimes it's as if he was there all along chained to my leg, keeping me in my box! But I have learned that fear is a poison dwarf that can only control you if you allow him to. Feel the fear and do it anyway. I remember being in Chicago a couple of years ago before an important keynote speech. I was on stage, in front of six hundred people, about to start and there, out of the corner of my eye, was Fear frowning over at me. I said to myself, 'You've come all this way? Well I suppose I can't stop you being here but you are not going to run this show!' And with that he was gone.

Fear is a poison dwarf that's hardwired; you can't have a procedure (like a Fear-ectomy) to remove him permanently! It is perfectly natural to experience fear, particularly when you set big goals that stretch and challenge you. The fears you experience when you go to the edge of your limit of capability can actually cause those limits to expand. Seneca, the Stoic philosopher, wrote that 'it is not because things are difficult that we do not dare; it is because we do not dare that they are difficult.'

Fear needs to be faced and the best antidotes to fear are security, courage and inner confidence. Remember that courage is not the absence of fear but the willingness to walk through your fear in pursuit of a goal that is important to you. Don't let fear be a roadblock to achieving your goals and dreams; instead look on it as a stepping stone to your future success. By having the confidence to face your fears, you can start to realise so much more of your creative potential and happiness.

What fears in your life might be holding you back? How much of your fear makes sense and is reasonable or rational? How great could you be if you could rise above your fears?

Envy

Aristotle once described envy as pain caused by the good fortune of others. Envy is a really resentful emotion that I call the green-eyed dwarf! Envy can cause what I call 'compareitis'; the crick in your neck from looking over your shoulder at other people with a sense of distress, comparing yourself to others, and in some way coming up short. It means wanting some trait that another person has (good looks, wealth, material possessions) and wishing that they didn't have it either. Envy starts with emptiness on the inside which brings on emotional pain, and a lowered sense of self-esteem and self-worth. *Schadenfreude* describes a gloating feeling experienced by seeing someone else suffer, which is often triggered by envy. The polar opposite to this feeling is *Mudita,* a Hindu term meaning delight at the good fortune of others.

Today's world is full of entitled demanders, whiners, complainers – people who want it all and want it all now. These people sense that someone owes them so that when they receive something, it is not a gift but their right. Instead of looking within for improvement and being grateful, they look outside themselves, comparing and competing with others. They are not running their own race; they want to reap but not to sow. This culture of entitlement promotes the Seven Poison Dwarfs, especially Envy.

In his essay on 'Self-Reliance', the American writer Ralph Waldo Emerson wrote that there is a time in every man's education when he arrives at the conviction that envy is ignorance. So watch out for the poison dwarf called Envy – just waiting for a chance to poison your thinking, creative potential and happiness. Putting on my medical hat for a minute, I believe the best antidote to the green-eyed poison dwarf called Envy is a healthy dose of gratitude, dispensed regularly. It is simply not possible to feel envious and grateful at the same time. Just try it and see for yourself!

Envy is often triggered by what I call the scarcity mentality: the belief in zero-sum games, whereby one person's gain means another person's loss. But happiness is a positive sum game, a win-win where your commitment to being happier can benefit everyone around you.

Anger

Anger is a very important poison dwarf, readying you for action just like the fight or flight response, the emotion that fuels violence. When you feel the emotion of anger you can fight injustice and protect what you value, right wrongs, and bring about needed change in the world. Over 2,300 years ago, Aristotle highlighted in *The Nicomachean Ethics* how easy becoming angry really is, but that to be angry with the right person, to the right degree, at the right time, for the right purpose, and in the right way is not easy. And it isn't! Misplaced anger can cause so much collateral damage that I think of anger as the great destroyer. There is an old Buddha saying that 'getting angry with another person is like throwing hot coals with bare hands; both people get burned.' Over the years I have met patients so consumed with anger (whether from real or perceived injustices) that it can quite literally destroy them unless or until they learn how to let go of it.

The boomerang effect is the age-old maxim that what goes around comes around. What you express becomes impressed, so if you express negatively towards others the strongest dose tends to come back to you. In terms of your happiness and emotional well-being, you really do reap what you sow. You may have encountered a situation in your life whereby a friend, work colleague or loved one has been in a row with you; you feel angry and annoyed, they have made you 'so mad.' What's more, you feel you were so right; so entitled to hold on to that anger and annoyance. So you stay angry after the argument because it shows other people just how angry and right you were. Maybe you feel that letting go of that anger may allow the other person to win. Sometimes you simply hold on to it to justify your entitlement to be right. However, nothing could be further from the truth. Whatever the source, inappropriate anger can cause so much psychological distress and emotional pain, triggering many of the other poison dwarfs, especially Anxiety and Fear. Worse still, holding on to inappropriate anger can be a hollow victory that comes at a price; your own physical health, psychological fitness and emotional well-being.

Anger and angina (heart pain) share the same root word (ankh). Confucius wrote that an angry man is always full of poison. This close connection between misplaced anger and all that negativity coursing through your veins like a poison has been recognised for thousands of years as damaging for your heart and physical health.

Perhaps one of the worst ways to deal with anger is by venting or expressing your anger to those around you; even the perceived short-term gain may be a false dawn. Rather than extinguishing the flame, venting of anger is far more likely to pour petrol onto the fire! Collateral damage to those around you can make them sick in the short term because of the contagion effect of negative emotion and may, as a result, damage an important relationship or friendship. Understanding this handicapping potential of inappropriate anger can allow you to better understand the Chinese proverb that if you are patient in one moment of anger, you will escape a hundred days of sorrow!

Anxiety

The poison dwarf called Anxiiety is closely connected to Fear and is often seen clinging onto his coat tails; in fact you rarely see one of these poison dwarfs without the other. Anxiety is considered to be a normal reaction to a stressful event or situation and is an emotion that everyone feels at one time or another. It may help you to deal with a demanding situation by prompting you to cope with it or alerting you to proceed with caution. A certain amount of anxiety or good stress is necessary for you to perform close to your potential. It can get you into the zone and revved up to perform at your best whether at work or on the sports field. But there is a fine line between the healthy performance-related anxiety that supports you in performing at your best and the stress that turns to distress once the perceived demands on you exceed your ability to cope. When this happens, the poison dwarf called Anxiety appears.

The Anxiety dwarf often appears as a result of dysfunctional thinking patterns, like all-or-nothing, black-cloud or must-do thinking. Anxiety about past events can trigger guilt and regret whereas anxiety about the future can lead to overwhelming worry or the illusion of control over future events, either real or imagined. Pessimistic thinking patterns can trigger anxiety and lead on to mild depression.

Anxiety becomes a poison dwarf when he interferes with daily activities and sleep; when he becomes a persistent and pervasive sense of being ill at ease that is unrelenting and unconnected to any single problem. Physical symptoms and signs caused by the Anxiety dwarf may include stomach upset, fatigue, difficulty sleeping, sweating, trembling hands, and restlessness.

The Anxiety dwarf is the chief reason for the tsunami of drugs (like Xanax, Valium and Stilnoct), prescribed by doctors and popped by patients throughout the Western world on a daily basis, so often resulting in tolerance, dependence and addiction. Whenever you have a situation in your life that makes you feel anxious and negative, you are giving away ownership and control of your emotional health to someone else. And when you allow someone or something outside of you to control how you feel, you lose your edge and leak valuable emotional energy.

Guilt

Everyone is imperfect, and you live in an imperfect world. If you are like most people, there are certain things you did or didn't do, said or didn't say which have caused a sense of regret. The Guilt dwarf, in small doses, can be helpful to keep you on track in life, following your values and moral compass. But the poison dwarf called Guilt can be a great destroyer of emotional energy, tying you up in knots where you lose no matter what! Guilt can be emotionally paralysing, arising when you believe you have done something wrong by your own standards in life or the standards of others. With the Guilt dwarf you may believe you have violated a moral standard, and you take full responsibility for that violation. Societies over the centuries have used Guilt (and Shame) to control, condition and coerce children (and adults) to behave as expected. Guilt can tie you up in knots and leave you feeling unworthy and miserable.

Guilt can be a losing battle; a powerful inner conflict where you lose no matter what you do, a real lose-lose! Excessive guilt is one of the biggest destroyers of self-esteem, creativity and personal happiness. He can become a relentless source of self-induced suffering, resulting in blame and self-hatred. Staying consumed with the Guilt dwarf keeps you stuck in a past of punishment, preventing you from moving forward in a positive and productive way. It can lead to self-disgust, depression, and a downward spiral of negativity.

This Guilt dwarf can pop up anywhere, anytime. I sometimes think of him as like the morning after the night before, when you indulged yourself with a big slice of chocolate cake after a late dinner. You stand on the weighing scales in your bathroom and there he is, sitting on your shoulder, literally weighing you down with negativity.

How to avoid the traps set by the Guilt dwarf!

- Use your journal to become more aware of the common guilt triggers and thinking patterns in your work, life and relationships. Remember that awareness precedes change.

- Understand your own needs and be honest about how you feel. Open up your heart so that you can really appreciate what is best for you rather than what you have been conditioned to believe.

- Become more accepting. Often in life there is no right or wrong, only experiences to learn from.

- Stop judging and start living, learning and growing.

- Trust yourself more. Take responsibility for your thoughts, feelings and actions. Be willing to apologise and stop doing something you really regret. Otherwise, dispense with guilt and don't let the poison dwarf called Guilt rule your life.

Shame

Shame is a self-conscious and emotionally highly destructive poison dwarf that tends to skulk around in your mind; it is often triggered by an inner sense of unworthiness, regret or inadequacy. Shame makes you want to hide, to stick your head in the sand. This can deaden the feeling of being really human which can lead to an outpouring of other poison dwarfs and generally toxic trends. As Benjamin Franklin wrote in 1734 in *Poor Richards Almanac:* 'Whatever is begun in anger ends in shame!'

Without a strong emotional bank account, Shame has the power to overwhelm you and leave you feeling empty and humiliated. Rejection or disapproval from others, feelings of inferiority or inadequacy can trigger feelings of Shame. This is a poison dwarf that can seriously damage your self-esteem and sense of self-worth, leading to self-hatred and lack of self-confidence.

Shame is not the same as Guilt though I think of them both as being like Siamese twins! Guilt is what you do, have done or will do. It's about your actions, a focus on behaviour. 'I did something bad.' Shame is about who you really are as a person, usually a negative focus upon oneself: 'I am a bad person. I am not good enough. I am not lovable.' Whereas you will be more likely to open up, admit and talk about Guilt or a situation that has triggered guilty feelings, you will be far less likely to talk about Shame in a similar vein. Shame tends to be concealed and hidden from others; unlike Guilt there is no distinction between the action and the self. Perhaps the best way to gain freedom from the poison dwarf called Shame is to face him squarely in the eye. Sometimes counselling or talking treatment in a psychologically safe space can help you to examine the unexpressed feelings and vulnerabilities that led to Shame. Start living a life consistent with your values, a reflection of your true authentic self. Learn to overcome Shame by building your empathy and self-esteem, becoming more compassionate and building greater connectivity with others.

Sadness

Sadness is a normal emotional response to many life events such as a significant loss, major life disappointment or the death of a loved one. It creates a desire to be inward-looking, to withdraw from life and everyday activities. Feeling sad at times is part and parcel of being human and the experience of sadness is common to all cultures. Even saying goodbye to someone you care about can trigger sadness.

Sadness can be a very primitive response to keep people closer to home when they are vulnerable, thereby keeping them safer. Sadness can allow you the opportunity to mourn a loss, to understand the implications and meaning for one's life. While sadness often results from a life event or change you didn't expect, it can create the psychological space for reflection and, in time, renewal and new beginnings. In this way, sadness can allow you to grow as a person, motivate you to deal with a situation and emotionally enrich your life. The yin and yang of life means that experiencing sadness can help you better appreciate the power of love.

As a poison dwarf, Sadness can be associated with feelings of disillusionment, despondency and despair. You may experience several of the other poison dwarfs especially Guilt and Anxiety. As sadness deepens it can lower mood and overlap closely with symptoms of depression. When this happens sadness becomes unmanageable. You may experience some or all of the following symptoms of depression which should prompt you to seek appropriate medical advice and support:

- Persistent sadness, emptiness, feelings of guilt, hopelessness or helplessness;
- Restlessness, irritability, short fuse;
- Difficulty in concentrating, decision-making or remembering;
- Loss of interest or enthusiasm for hobbies or pleasurable activities, including sex;
- Withdrawal socially;
- Sleep disturbance: this may include difficulty getting to sleep, staying asleep or early morning wakening;
- Tiredness, loss of energy, feeling slowed down;
- Change in appetite, and associated weight loss or gain;
- Persistent physical symptoms such as headaches, bowel disorders, chronic pain;
- Passive death wishes or thoughts about suicide.

Tips for managing your Sadness dwarf

- Better out than in! Don't suppress or fight sadness, be willing to express your tears, cry if you feel like it. Don't drive him underground.
- Don't get stuck; know when your sadness is crossing over into possible depression and seek appropriate help

and support; remember you are not alone.

- ۶ Be nicer to yourself; don't beat yourself up with unrealistic expectations or make important decisions when you are sad.

- ۶ Look on the bright side, use the Sadness dwarf to gain a new perspective; there can be a complex sort of joy in sadness, remember how much great art, music and poetry is inspired by sadness.

These Seven Poison Dwarfs (Fear, Envy, Anger, Anxiety, Guilt, Shame and Sadness) tend to hunt in packs. They are joined at the hip so you rarely see one without at least several others close behind. Nothing makes them happier than the opportunity to get into your mind and dance their destructive dance. They will cause headache, heartache and real emotional havoc. And they are everywhere. So when you sit down with your family for breakfast remember those dwarfs are never far from the table. Likewise at work whether in the boardroom, the office or factory floor, the dwarfs are just waiting for their chance to come out and run riot, to demonise, depress and detract from your ability to think positively!

The poison dwarfs are so strong and powerful that they can clog up the emotional wiring in your brain and cause an emotional hangover. By holding onto the poison dwarfs, you give away ownership and control of your emotional well-being. As a result, you lose your edge and leak valuable emotional energy. The problem with the poison dwarfs is that wallowing in them will never allow you to realise your dreams, develop those special relationships, or reach your potential. They will keep you stuck, choked up with negativity, wallowing in self-righteous pity and causing so much damage to your emotional well-being and happiness. So watch out, be careful! If you don't have enough positivity to counteract those poison dwarfs, they can put you on a real downward spiral.

Dysphoria, a psychological term for feeling bad, is temporary bad mood weather that affects everybody. But a more pervasive climate change is when you experience despair. Fear and Anxiety can cascade into negative stress (distress) which can mushroom into a sort of hopeless Sadness mixed with the flames of Anger which in turn can breed Envy, Guilt and Shame. Wallowing extinguishes the flame of positivity, putting you on a downward spiral to despair.

I call wallowing the eighth poison dwarf: where you persistently push the self-destruct button, preventing you from realising your dreams or reaching your potential. As you become consumed with your own negativity you can become a poison dwarf yourself which can lead you all the way to rock bottom, weighed down in negativity, focused on what you have not, and who you are not.

Breaking Free

The poison dwarfs are real for everyone; they've been in your life (and mine) and are part of the fullness of human experience. Unchecked, they have the potential to undermine your happiness and seriously damage your health and well-being. But you can choose not to let them become the stars of the show by not giving them any more attention than they deserve! Become more aware of them and the impact they are having in your life. Awareness allows you to make better choices in terms of your emotional well-being, resulting in more of a sense of inner contentment and fulfilment.

Face your fears, allay your anxiety, address your anger. Let go of guilt, evade envy, soar above sadness and shame. Awareness of the destructive potential of the poison dwarfs can provide the opportunity to respond to them constructively as well as gaining more meaning from your experiences. They can also be a powerful catalyst for positive transformational change. But important and necessary though this strategy is, on its own this way of dealing with the poison dwarfs isn't enough to feel happy. In fact, you can put all those poison dwarfs back in their box, and still feel flat and empty, devoid of the spark so essential for happiness and well-being. The good news is they are not the only dwarfs in town. In the next chapter you will learn about the critical game-changing importance of the happy dwarfs in building sustainable happiness.

I remember reading a story about an old Cherokee Indian talking to his grandson about two wolves fighting an ongoing battle inside his head. One wolf represents evil: fear, envy, anger, anxiety, guilt, shame, sadness. The other represents goodness: love, joy, hope, interest, inspiration, enthusiasm, fun. The grandson looks into the wise eyes of his granddad and asks: 'Which wolf wins the battle?' And the granddad smiles lovingly at his grandson and says: 'The one you feed!'

Dharma is a term for the spiritual practice of the Buddha or universal spiritual law and the practice of *Dharma* is a constant battle within. The Sanskrit word *Dharma* means any action or understanding that protects you or holds you back from experiencing suffering, negativity and its causes. You have the power to choose which thoughts to focus on, which emotions to cultivate and which actions and behaviours will make up your day-to-day experiences. Your mind is a battleground and only you can write the script of your own particular battle. When you do, what will it read like?

Chapter 3
Seven Happy Dwarfs

My Auntie Dolores

I remember one sunny school day in June. I'm eight years old, skipping home through the fields at lunch time from my local primary school. That feeling of freedom, free as a bird, without a care in the world. Pushing in the front door which was always on the latch back then, skipping into the kitchen and there it was – a big box on the kitchen table covered in brown wrapping paper. As I got closer I could see the stamps on the top right-hand corner, the symbols of the American flag and George Washington. Handle with Care was franked in black and the handwriting, 'Master Mark Rowe.' 'Oh that's your Auntie Dolores', said my mother, as if I thought it could be anyone else.

Now I don't know if you had somebody special in your life growing up, someone kind, loving, understanding, someone who was always there for you when it really mattered. If you do or if you did, then I hope you know how lucky you were. You see Auntie Dolores was such a person for me. She was such a playful aunt to have, a wonderful person for celebrating

A PRESCRIPTION FOR HAPPINESS

birthdays, Christmas, Easter and occasions of every sort. She never missed one, either in person or via post.

Between the tape and the twine, opening the parcel was quite a procedure. Such excitement! Out came a black cassette recorder with a post-it on it that said 'play me.' I did and this is what I remember hearing: 'Good morning Brendan, Geraldine, Mark and Colman. Greetings from Washington DC where the weather is very hot, about 90 degrees. Gerald Ford is president at the moment but there is going to be an election next year. I hope Jimmy Carter gets in. He is a peanut farmer from the South but I think he is for the poor really. I went to the White House the other day. Work is going well, same ol' same ol'. Looking forward to seeing you all next year. Please send a tape back soon.' As an eight-year-old boy in 1970s Ireland, listening to her talking about her magical life in America was quite an experience for me. Back then we didn't even have a telephone and even if we had, the cost of transatlantic phone calls was quite prohibitive. As I listened to Auntie Dolores talking, I rummaged through the box and played with the polystyrene foam when to my amazement I discovered a second tape. It had her magic symbol on it, a red heart. When Dolores had finished talking I put this second tape carefully into the cassette recorder, pressed the play button and this is what I heard: 'Zip-a-dee-doo-dah, zip-a-dee-day; my oh my, what a wonderful day. Plenty of sunshine heading my way, zip-a-dee-doo-dah, zip-a-dee-day.' As a child Auntie Dolores had brought the zip-a-dee-doo-dah, that magical spirited sense of adventure, into my life. After she died, I looked again at our relationship – but this time through new eyes. I realised that the gifts she had given me were not contained in a brown box but were the priceless gifts of hope, inspiration, interest, enthusiasm, fun, joy and the giant of unconditional love – the Seven Happy Dwarfs!

Key Benefits of the Seven Happy Dwarfs

When you experience the happy dwarfs, changes in the brain and nervous system boost the levels of happy feel-good chemicals, bringing on the 'relaxation response'. This leads to a generalised sense of calm and contentment with less negative stress. You produce natural painkillers called endorphins (so-called because they are related to morphine) so your pain threshold goes up, while blood pressure and cortisol levels (the stress hormone) are lowered.

Dopamine release stimulates the pleasure and reward centres in the brain, so you get an immediate dose of pleasure; improving motivation, problem solving and your working memory. This enhances your social interactions and helps change your perspective on things.

Sometimes called 'the love hormone', oxytocin supports the 'tend and befriend' response. As you experience more positivity, you more easily form attachments, feel empathy, and express feelings of warmth, trust and compassion.

The happy dwarfs come from your thoughts, which is exciting because you have the power and ability to control your thoughts or more specifically which thoughts you give attention to! They are triggered not by your circumstances but by your interpretation of those circumstances. As a barometer of the amount of well-being and happiness in your life, the happy dwarfs enhance life satisfaction, enabling you to sparkle and shine like a diamond.

The happy dwarfs enable you to better focus on your goals and build those health-boosting habits. They support a stronger immune system (fewer colds), better sleep and lower blood pressure, keeping you healthier and protecting you against the ageing process. In fact their presence can lower the risk of many chronic illnesses. The happy dwarfs are life enhancing, adding years to your life as well as life to your years.

A PRESCRIPTION FOR HAPPINESS

The happy dwarfs build what is known as your emotional intelligence, the ability to be better tuned in to your own emotions, to better understand and relate to others and the situations in which you encounter them. This includes awareness of your own feelings, empathy and the art of listening, cooperating and resolving conflicts. Daniel Goleman from Harvard University, author of *Emotional Intelligence*, has highlighted that traditional IQ contributes only about 20 per cent to the factors that determine life success; other factors, including emotional intelligence, comprise the other 80 per cent. This makes sense as emotional intelligence helps you to build better relationships, the leading indicator of your happiness and well-being. The further up the career ladder you go, the more important emotional intelligence appears to become. Emotions are highly contagious and a key part of emotional intelligence is being able to manage the exchange of emotion in relationships; to make others feel good, appreciated and positive. Understanding that you all see things differently; taking the perspective of others on board; appreciating and valuing the differences.

The happy dwarfs build your sense of empathy, which is at the very heart of effective communication. The word 'empathy' comes from the Greek *empatheia*, 'feeling into', meaning the ability to feel or perceive what someone else is feeling. Empathy is all about *being* more rather than *knowing* more. Being more caring and considerate; being more emotionally attuned to the needs and feelings of others; being a better listener. As you become more empathic, you become more willing to reach out and support others. Empathy is an extension of self-awareness; as you become more attuned to your own thoughts, feelings and emotions, so you become more attuned to the feelings and emotions of others. This helps you to better understand the needs, wants and viewpoints of those people around you and to value the differences.

A PRESCRIPTION FOR HAPPINESS

Compassion is a sense of deep empathy; not just knowing but *feeling* the feelings of others. True compassion requires the courage to be vulnerable and to own your sense of vulnerability. Einstein said that true compassion was compassion for the whole of existence, for every last speck of dust within it; embracing all living creatures and the whole of nature in its beauty. Taking the time to be more compassionate and understanding of the perspectives of others will help you to become more creative, effective and emotionally secure. The happy dwarfs encourage your mind to really engage with life and to become pleasurably absorbed with everyday experiences.

One effect of these happy dwarfs is that, over time, they can build up your so-called 'emotional bank account', creating reserves of positivity that you can draw upon when a threat or opportunity presents itself. The happy dwarfs build your reservoirs of well-being, supporting psychological fitness, emotional as well as physical vitality and robust relationships.

The happy dwarfs help you to think bigger and better, more creatively and expansively. By transforming your thinking, you will be better able to problem solve and find more constructive solutions to the inevitable challenges you face in life. As a result, you will have a broader range of vision and be better able to tolerate uncertainty with more perspective; be able, in essence, to see both the wood and the trees!

The happy dwarfs provide the fairy dust that allows your imagination to flourish, strengthening innovation and creating new possibilities for you in your life. They can build your brain resources as you are more open to learning new things. Plato the philosopher emphasised how 'All learning has an emotional base.' As your memory is dependent on your mood, when you are in a good mood you will remember more positive events and associations, building your knowledge, memory and recall.

The happy dwarfs build your confidence in your interactions

with the world around you. They help you adapt better to the many challenges that life brings, adopt better coping strategies, and be more able to perform complex tasks. Change is the only constant in life, and can make you feel uncomfortable, insecure, and vulnerable. Change is inevitable; you can try to resist it or you can be proactive, roll with the punches and celebrate change for the wonderful opportunities it can bring. Embrace change! Wrap your mind, your arms and your future around it. The happy dwarfs can help you to acclimatise to change and open your mind to the new possibilities it can bring in its wake.

The happy dwarfs encourage a more open mindset. They invite you to be more open and receptive to new ideas; to people, places and situations; to new experiences and opportunities. They support different pathways and possibilities to achieve your goals. They open your mind and allow you to feel more connected to nature.

As your happy dwarfs kick in, you will become more sociable and friendly, helping you to build a broader network of social connections and friendships. Quite simply, when you are in a more positive mood people like you better and are more attracted to you. Being better liked builds trust and helps create the environment that makes relationships more likely to flourish.

The happy dwarfs build communication skills and support what I call the '5 Cs' of robust relationships:

- Communicating more clearly. Active listening; effective non-verbal communication skills such as maintaining eye contact, using hand gestures, facial expressiveness; empathy (listening with your heart).

- Controlling conflict constructively. Learning the skills of conflict resolution, responding effectively

to criticism, compromise (win-win), and the art of
compassion, valuing openness and building trust.

- ♌ Connectedness. Bringing you closer to the important people in your life, promoting the common ground, that sense of oneness; moving you from me to we; from me and you, to we and us!

- ♌ Clarifying. Being able to make clear requests and state your concerns in a non-emotional way. Showing the leadership to find more constructive ways of responding appropriately to the emotions in others.

- ♌ Copping on. Common sense is not always common action!

The happy dwarfs can prevent negative stress from worsening and can undo the damaging effects of stress. Provided they are present in the right numbers (ratio of at least three happy dwarfs to each poison dwarf), they can zap stress, make you less defensive and break the tight spell those poison dwarfs can cast on you. The happy dwarfs are contagious out to three degrees of separation. So your feeling happier doesn't just benefit you: happy dwarfs can jump, spread feelings of positivity and impact on the lives of those people around you; a real win-win-win.

The happy dwarfs support psychological fitness and more positive mental health, helping you to become more resilient, to bounce back from life's challenges and to smile in the face of adversity. Not to stick your head in the sand but to face the challenges of life head on, allowing you to reframe the dark clouds through the lens of the silver lining and rebound with realistic optimism. They foster acceptance and an increased sense of purpose in your life. The happy dwarfs are energising and empowering, encouraging you to be more honest and to focus on delayed gratification. They support your growth to become the person you are capable of becoming, the best possible version of yourself.

The happy dwarfs allow you to think, feel and behave at your best; to look at yourself and the world around you more positively and generously. They allow you to become more authentic and to grow, develop and evolve as a person. Authenticity radiates your inner core and heartfelt positivity enables you to reveal more of this to the world. Having a positive attitude towards life makes you happier. And whatever way you choose to measure it – whether by the quality of your relationships, accomplishments, or health – a positive attitude towards life enables you to become more successful.

And so, let's get to know the good guys, these Seven Happy Dwarfs.

Love

Love is the supreme positive emotion. Perhaps the greatest force in the universe, Love is a happy dwarf that allows you to become more fully alive in the present moment. Love is sharing and caring, supporting and comforting, and so much more. Love is by far the biggest of all the happy dwarfs, a giant in disguise, characterised by attachment, caring and passionate commitment. He can refer to a variety of different feelings, states and attitudes. These range from pleasure ('I loved that cake'), interpersonal attraction ('I love my partner'), the emotional closeness of familial love, the platonic love that defines friendship, or the passionate desire and intimacy of romantic love. Love can be experienced in acts of kindness, generosity and self-sacrifice.

As the polar opposite of hate, love heals, encourages, inspires and forgives. Martin Luther King wrote: 'Darkness cannot drive out darkness, only light can do that; hate cannot drive out hate, only love can do that.'

Receiving the gift of Love (from the people who love you and let you love them) can be transformational and a sort of magical glue in long-term relationships. As Lao, the ancient Chinese philosopher, once said: 'Being deeply loved by someone gives you strength, while loving someone deeply gives you courage.'

Love multiplies like a magic penny and is a kind of passionate commitment that enhances feelings of safety and security. Love is life's greatest blessing, love is timeless, love conquers all.

Hindus believe that you are layered in shrink-wrapped sheaths, like onion layers, called *samskaras*. Each layer represents a form of emotional pain or bad karma and your challenge is to break through these sheaths so that you can become a fully mature, conscious adult. The innermost part of the onion represents your heart, or pure love.

Loving-kindness meditation is a powerful way to increase feelings of love, care and compassion; not only for you but for important others in your life. This is similar to mindful meditation in that traditional loving-kindness meditation also has mantras or phrases that you repeat to yourself.

'May you feel safe, may you feel happy, may you feel healthy, may you live with ease' is a common phrase used in loving-kindness meditation. The main difference is one of emphasis: on the heart rather than the mind. The focus is not so much on quietening the mind as on generating warm, compassionate thoughts about yourself and others. These thoughts are initially directed towards your own heart and then outwards to others, firstly to those you love and care about and subsequently beyond that to the whole world. Your heart becomes the focal point to see, hear and sense feelings of compassion and love. As a result you experience more feelings of love, joy, hope, peacefulness and serenity. As you allow your life to be enriched with some of the benefits of loving-kindness meditation, you develop a greater awareness and sense of connectedness with others and your overall satisfaction with life is enhanced.

When did the happy dwarf called Love captivate you? Who do you love, and who loves you?

Joy

Joy is a happy dwarf that empowers you to succeed and comes from knowing you are living the life you were meant to live. Joy can be defined as a feeling of great pleasure, happiness or elation; it allows you to feel confident, capable, lovable, powerful and fulfilled. Thich Nhat Hanh, the wisdom monk, has written that sometimes your joy is the source of your smile, but sometimes your smile can be the source of your joy. Joy radiates brightness and lights you up on the inside with an inner glow. Joy flows from your heart, just like peace and love.

Sharing joy sparks off joy in others and is highly contagious. There is a wise saying that if you share sorrow, you half the sorrow, whereas if you share joy, you double the joy!

Joy can be an instantaneous moment in time when everything is going to plan, and joy encapsulates how you feel – the smile of your newborn baby, a special moment with a loved one or family member. Joy is choosing to look up not down, and represents something wonderful, not woeful. Joy is your inner light that allows you to reconnect with a power greater than yourself. Despite all the wonderful attributes of this happy dwarf, Joy has traditionally been mistrusted as being too good to be true! Ironically, Freud wrote about twenty-four volumes of human psychology without managing to mention joy even once!

Many people think and believe that Joy is something that can only be experienced when everything is going right in your life. Not so! The old Greek word, *soteria,* refers to your high irrational joys, a name that came from the feast held upon deliverance from death. The irony is that joy is so often linked to pain and often follows relief from your worst fears.

This paradox of joy (the bitter-sweet) means that without the pain of separation, it is impossible to fully experience the joy of reunion; without the pain of effort, it is impossible to fully experience the joy of reward; without the pain of rejection, it is impossible to fully experience the joy of acceptance.

A more sustained form of joy is serenity, or a deep sense of peacefulness about what you are experiencing. This is being able to let go and lap it up. You are savouring in the moment, without any guilt/regrets about the past or worries/concerns about the future. Strolling down a sandy beach, relaxing with a nice cup of tea, or an invigorating massage are great examples of ways to experience serenity. It is a mindful state, when everything is so right, when you say to yourself: 'I must do this more often.'

How you can bring more of the Joy dwarf into your life?

- Be more joyful. It's your choice. Reach out and bring more joy and happiness into the lives of others.

- Jump for joy. Be more mindful and allow yourself to find the hidden joy in every experience. Understand that you deserve to experience Joy. It is your nature, who you are on the inside.

- Celebrate the moments in your life and transform those moments into lifelong memories. Sometimes the small things really are the big things. Taking the time to celebrate builds joy and a sense of fulfilment. So take action and think of something you can celebrate this week. What big or little thing have you accomplished? Who is deserving of a little celebrating right now?

☙ Ask yourself what brings you the happy dwarf called Joy. Perhaps the joy of anticipation, connecting with nature, the birds singing, spending more time with children, looking for smiles, listening to music. Write a list of those things that bring you joy and heartfelt delight.

Hope

The happy dwarf called Hope comes from your ability as a human being to imagine the future, specifically a more realistic positive future. Despair is the polar opposite of Hope (the word despair comes from the Latin word *disperare*, meaning to be without hope).

When I think of the happy dwarf called Hope, I'm reminded of a fable about four lighting candles on a table in a room. These candles flickered and burned brightly as the serenity of their shadows brought an overwhelming sense of calm to the space. You could almost hear them speak. And then they did:

The first candle said, 'My name is Peace but these days, with so much turmoil in the world, very few want to keep me lit.' Then Peace's flame slowly diminished and went out completely. Next the second candle said, 'I am Faith, but these days, the world has changed so much that I am no longer indispensable.' A gentle breeze blew softly on it and, after a brief flicker, it was gone. Sadly the third candle spoke, 'I am the giant of unconditional love, but I just haven't got the strength to stay lit any longer; even though hate can never drive out hate, people tend to put me aside and don't appreciate how important I am.' And with that he was gone.

Just then a young boy entered the room and with tear-filled eyes asked, 'Where are you gone to? Weren't you supposed to be here until the end?' And with that he started to cry.

Just then the fourth candle, who had been silent up to now, spoke, 'Don't cry little boy, wipe away your tears. My name is Hope and, as long as I'm around, we can relight the other three candles!'

Hope can build a foundation stone of real possibility in your life. When you stop hoping you start settling. Hope allows you to believe in all the actions you need to bring your dreams to reality. Hope is the happy dwarf that fosters your belief in a positive outcome related to events and circumstances in your life. Hope can energise you, elevate you, and encourage you to believe that everything can work out for the best. Hope is closely related to Inspiration; both encourage you to look forward to a brighter future.

Hope is a patient, kind and comforting emotion; it allows you to understand that tomorrow or the day after tomorrow may be a better day, that this too shall pass.

In many respects Hope is a happy dwarf that symbolises possibility. Hope is a beacon of light for the possibility that things can improve, a belief in possibility itself, in the idea that you can do it. Hope for the future gives power to the present, sustaining and motivating you to work towards your goals.

Hope faces adversity squarely in the eye and turns that very same adversity into opportunity; the darkest night into the dawn. Hope can transform suffering into manageable pain. Hope is honest. Hope springs eternal; a reminder of the possibility that as in winter gardens, the seeds of spring renewal have already been planted. Hope fosters resilience, real ambition and resourcefulness and has been recognised as a key constituent of emotional intelligence. Hope is the belief that you have both the will and the way to achieve your goals. And having high levels of hope can give you the strength, stamina and steely resolve to do just that.

Inspiration

This is a happy dwarf that can literally put the spirit of life in you. When I think of Inspiration, I recall the writings of Patanjali, the author of *Yoga Sutras*, who lived in India over 2,000 years ago.

'When you are inspired by some great
purpose, some extraordinary project,
all your thoughts break their bonds;
Your mind transcends limitations,
your consciousness expands in every direction,
and you find yourself in a new, great
and wonderful world.
Dormant forces, faculties and talents
become alive, and you discover yourself
to be a greater person by far
than you ever dreamed
yourself to be.'

Inspiration is a happy dwarf that involves the process of being mentally stimulated by a deep desire to do or feel something creative and make a positive change. This feeling can be triggered by experiencing or witnessing unanticipated acts of human kindness or compassion. As the word literally translates, Inspiration is a happy dwarf that takes your breath away.

Inspiration draws you in and makes you want to better yourself, to express more of your own unique potential. It pulls you away from your sense of self-obsession and towards a sense of transcendence. Inspiration encourages you to be a force for positive change; to do good in the world, to do what is right for others.

Awe is closely related to Inspiration. Awe is a description of that transcendent moment when, overwhelmed with goodness, you stop in your tracks. Awe gives you that feeling of being part of something much greater than yourself. You can be awed by nature, natural events, or new experiences unfolding like I was in the Raphael Rooms in Rome.

Ways to invite the Inspiration dwarf into your daily life

- When do you feel extraordinary? When in your life did you last experience the dwarf called Inspiration? Use your journal to record those activities that make you feel inspired, no matter what they are.

- Open your eyes and choose to see the world around you in a new light. Witnessing amazing feats of intellect, strength and agility can lead to inspiration. Connect with nature. Be inspired by being in the presence of great natural beauty: walk barefoot on the beach, watch the sunset or gaze at the starry night. Tune in to the Olympics to watch an athlete set a new personal best and see genuine human excellence transcending everyday experience. Visit an art gallery and immerse yourself in its wonder and beauty. As Picasso wrote: 'Art washes away the dust from the soul of everyday life.'

- Read an uplifting story about somebody who succeeds against all the odds. Read the biographies of great leaders, or inspirational quotes from philosophers. Connect with someone who is taking action to make the world a better place. Don't wait for Inspiration to start. Start and the happy dwarf called Inspiration will find you.

Enthusiasm

The word *enthusiasm* originated from the Greek word *entheos*, meaning 'to be filled with God, in ecstasy.' In modern times enthusiasm implies an attitude of engagement, of larger-than-life excitement in a particular subject. As a happy dwarf, Enthusiasm is particularly contagious, with a bubbly vivacious spirit that puts a spring in your step and brings a sparkle to your eyes. Enthusiasm is one of the most attractive qualities a person can have and is a powerful form of communication. People can sense your enthusiasm and see you in a more positive light, which in turn will open up more opportunities for you. For me, one of the keys to giving a great talk or workshop is being really enthusiastic.

The Enthusiasm dwarf energises, engenders success and emboldens you through life's challenges. Enthusiasm can give you more confidence and help you to keep going when faced with challenging tasks. He can give you the drive to pursue a particular passion, and a willingness to go the extra mile, beyond the normal boundaries of possibility. Enthusiasm helps you to get more things done with better results. To be more effective in the world, choose to be more enthusiastic, positive and optimistic. Having more enthusiasm in your life is a great way to achieve fulfilment. He gives Joy a helping hand and puts Fear back in his box where he belongs!

Enthusiasm is so essential if you want to accomplish anything of value; nothing great was ever achieved without it. He can bring a sense of pride from achievement and a sense of purpose into your everyday experiences, especially when this is accompanied by a sense of healthy humility.

Enthusiasm is great fun and makes life so much more enjoyable. Enthusiasm is like the conductor of the orchestra of happy dwarfs, facilitating positive change, building confidence and real contentment.

How to strengthen your Enthusiasm dwarf

- ✤ To bring more enthusiasm into your life, act more enthusiastically! If knowledge is power, then enthusiasm is the switch! Don't wait for favourable circumstances to become enthusiastic; instead bring in the Enthusiasm dwarf and circumstances will grow more favourable. If you are at the start of an event or activity, let yourself think that this is both the first and last time you will have this experience; just watch your level of enthusiasm skyrocket!

- ✤ Be more of a leader. This takes energy, engagement and discipline. Become more enthusiastic and remember it's your choice. Don't be a spectator in life. Become a participant and spend more time and energy doing those things you are passionate about. Do what you love and love what you do! Having a plan of setting and working towards your goals can foster a sense of pride in yourself and those accomplishments. This can result in terrific excitement and a deep sense of satisfaction.

- ✤ Be proud of your achievements. Those things you are proud of are worthy of having enthusiasm for. Be patient and maintain a positive outlook, even in the face of so-called failure. Use your experiences as an opportunity to learn and draw inspiration from your successes. Commit yourself to the journey of mastery; knowing that every day you are improving is a wonderful way to build enthusiasm.

✎ Take more exercise which will enhance your energy, your enthusiasm and your vitality levels. Be more creative and innovative; new ideas spark enthusiasm while enthusiasm creates new ideas. Surround yourself with enthusiastic people because enthusiasm is so contagious! Ask yourself, are you bringing enough enthusiasm into your life?

Interest

Closely connected to Inspiration, Interest is a happy dwarf that seldom receives the same attention as some of the others. Interest encourages you to explore new ideas, to be open to new possibilities. Interest is the emotion of being curious, developing a love of learning, being on the lookout for activities you may enjoy. Being interested can invigorate you, intrigue you and invite you to unlock more of your creative talents and potential. The Interest dwarf can make you appreciate more of what it means to be more fully alive in the moment.

A strong sense of interest and curiosity can help fulfilment. Notice how children view the world through eyes of wonder and live out of their imagination, not their memory. Pablo Picasso wrote how it took him four years to paint like Raphael but a lifetime to paint like a child; that every child is an artist but the challenge is how to remain an artist and childlike when he grows up.

The Interest dwarf fosters creativity and a sense of

fascination. Creativity can be cultivated through the 'I'll try anything once' attitude. You can become more creative by coming up with clever ways to solve everyday problems or pursuing hobbies and interests that matter to you.

Ways to develop your Interest dwarf

- Stretch yourself. Have the courage to step out of your comfort zone, try new things, and take on new challenges. Consider exposing yourself to different viewpoints and embrace new ideas. Talk to unusual people, who may have completely different backgrounds to you, and appreciate the benefits of learning from their experiences.

- Be creative and redesign your own environment at home or at work. Visit art galleries or exhibitions of creative work. Become more connected, expansive and creative in your thinking. Journey to the place where the greatest learning occurs!

- Be more curious. Read a new book and awaken to new ideas. Read an article or editorial on a topic you know little or nothing about. Listen to different forms of music. Take a new route to work, lunch with someone different. Learn a new language. Cook an exotic meal in the evening. Ask yourself, when did you last experience the Interest dwarf?

Fun

The Fun dwarf helps you to recharge your battery and replenish your energy. Fun, laughter and a good sense of humour are some of the most powerful antidotes to discouragement, disillusionment and pessimism. Fun can give you greater zest for life, more pep in your step, more of that 'zip-a-dee-doo-dah' feeling.

Fun is a happy dwarf that can be a great teacher. Play can teach you how to lose while playing to win, how to tolerate risk and uncertainty, how to build empathy and those critical skills of social survival. Children are energetic, full of enthusiasm and naturally embrace the Fun dwarf. Children play because it feels good to play, plain and simple. But the Fun dwarf also supports their growth and learning about rough and tumble and the rules of social interaction. You are hardwired to be playful because it is such an important survival tool.

The Fun dwarf is not just for children or the young at heart; he is for everyone. George Bernard Shaw, the nineteenth-century Irish playwright, wrote that 'we don't stop playing because we grow old; we grow old because we stop playing.' The Fun dwarf can keep you younger physically and psychologically. Unfortunately, people can become laden down with deadlines, timetables and responsibilities in life, losing sight of those things that really put a smile on your face and the sunshine of youthful play. There is a Fun dwarf inside you just looking for the space and opportunity to be heard and seen. Nurture your Fun dwarf and he will pay you the dividend of a rich emotional life.

How to support your Fun dwarf?

- Learn how to channel your energies wholeheartedly into something new, something you are passionate about or someone you love. Become more spontaneous and do things just for the sheer delight of doing them. Replenish your energy and explore new ways to reconnect with your Fun dwarf.

- Spend more time with children who are naturally

playful and approach life with excitement and curiosity. Play with a pet; play with a puppy; plug into their energy and playful spirit. Play more games. Colour monkeys purple instead of brown! Learn to be free, to unwind. Dance, loosen up, laugh at yourself.

- Have you enough of the Fun dwarf in your life? When was the last time you did something for the first time? What captured your imagination when you were eight years old? What brought you excitement at that age? Reconnect with your inner child! Make more time for fun in your life.

Give Your Happy Dwarfs a Boost – With Laughter

The sound of laughter can be just the emotional tonic to tell your brain to bring on more of those happy dwarfs. Laughter can boost your energy, is a strong antidote to the stresses and strains of life and provides powerful medicine for the mind, body and soul. Laughter can help your sleep and induce a general sense of relaxation, allowing you to produce natural painkillers (endorphins) and increase your tolerance for pain. It builds up your emotional bank account with feel-good chemicals in your brain, providing a buffer against disagreements and resentments. Laughter is a great way to power up your psychological fitness and is a great stress buster. Laughter causes release of the happy hormones in the brain that can relax your muscles, strengthen the immune system and help protect you from the damaging effects of stress.

Laughter can dissolve the poison dwarfs, especially Anxiety and Fear, and better support your ability to cope with challenging situations. It fosters a sense of realistic optimism, and enhances resilience.

Laughter shared can be a bond that builds relationships, promotes teamwork and improves your quality of life. Laughter is a social activity and you are far more likely to laugh when you are with other people than when you are alone. Building your sense of connection with other people and feeling closer to friends and family may be the main health benefits of laughter.

Laugh each day to keep heart attack away? Just as an apple a day keeps the doctor away, so laughing may be good for your heart (as the literal meaning of the word light-hearted might suggest!).

Set yourself the goal of bringing more laughter into your life on a regular basis. Make time for laughter in everyday conversations. Practise laughing more – practice makes improvement. Keep funny movies or comedy shows on standby for when you need them. Check out laughter yoga! Founded by Indian doctor Madan Kataria, (who is popularly known as the 'guru of giggling'), this combines breathing and stretching exercises with laughter-inducing clapping and chanting.

Spend more time with friends who make you laugh. Remember their playful point of view. Laughter is highly contagious, perhaps more than even a sneeze or a wheeze. Make time for your inner child to play. Laugh and the world laughs with you. Learn to laugh at yourself, and see how your stress melts away. Let laughter be your low calorie medicine. Never take yourself too seriously. No-one else will!

The Importance of Balance

'Fear less, hope more

Sigh less, breathe more

Hate less, love more

A PRESCRIPTION FOR HAPPINESS

And all good things will be yours.'
SWEDISH PROVERB

Are you bringing enough of the happy dwarfs into your life? What about minimising the impact of those poison dwarfs? I don't mean denying your problems or sticking your head in the sand. It's important to acknowledge your challenges and stresses and a poison dwarf or two can have their place but they need to be kept under tight control or else they can run riot.

You might think, as I once did, that you need one happy dwarf to balance or counteract one poison dwarf. Kind of makes sense! In recent years educators have spoken about the 'critical sandwich': couching a piece of negative feedback in between two bits of positive feedback to minimise its impact. Now it's accepted that you need much more than that. Negative feedback can be so powerful and can leave such a strong hangover that you need lots of happy dwarfs available to counteract those poison dwarfs!

Pioneering work by leading psychologist Barbara Fredrickson described in her book *Positivity* has shown that, to truly flourish and live at your best, you need at least three positive emotions or happy dwarfs to counteract each negative emotion or poison dwarf. That is the tipping point for emotional well-being and Fredrickson's research suggests that only about twenty percent of people actually achieve this ratio. Most people have only a ratio of about 2:1 and are plodding along, far from their best (a ratio of 1:1 or less indicates mental health issues like depression). So if you get up in the morning and you have a row at home, then drive into work and have a grumpy interaction with one of your colleagues, you may get to coffee break two down, by which time, to get back on track, you need *six* happy dwarfs just to counteract those two poison dwarfs. No wonder so many people are struggling.

And in your key relationships, the ratio is even higher at 5:1. Five happy dwarfs to counteract one poison dwarf! So just as getting your 'five-a-day' quota of fruit and vegetables is essential for optimal physical health, you need your emotional 'five a day' to keep the emotional well-being of your key relationships in the best possible condition.

In recent years, smoking cigarettes and tobacco products have, quite rightly, been banned from the workplace because it was recognised, through painstaking research, that passive smoking and side-stream smoke are so toxic for your health and increase the risk of cancer, occupational asthma and many other conditions. Well, the poison dwarfs can be just as bad for your physical health, for your energy levels and emotional vitality, as smoking cigarettes! Furthermore, they are highly contagious! So, on health and well-being grounds, I believe that negative emotion should also be banned from the workplace and house; left at the front door of your organisation and your home (whether at breakfast or in the bedroom).

Without exception, the poison dwarfs show up in your life and play their role in the totality and fullness of the range of human experiences. In fact, you may not survive long without some of them! Remember anger can allow you to fight injustice and protect what you value; fear can be mission critical for your survival. You have to live in the real world and the poison dwarfs are real. But you can reduce needless negativity in your life and learn to put some of those poison dwarfs back in their box. The key is to offset the harmful effects of negative emotion by ramping up the positivity levels in your life so that the ratio of happy to poison dwarfs remains at least 3:1 (and at least 5:1 in your key interpersonal relationships).

This ratio is not 3:0; negativity has its role to play. But those poison dwarfs need to be counterbalanced with enough positivity. So step up to the plate and become the best possible version of yourself that you can be. Develop big picture thinking; small daily improvements over time can transform your life. It is all about balance. The right ratio of happy to poison Dwarfs leads to a win-win scenario, cultivating better physical health, psychological fitness, stronger relationships, and overall greater happiness and well-being. Remember at the end of the day it's your choice; your emotional vitality and happiness are up to you!

Chapter 4
The Journal – Fine-tuning Your Psychological Fitness

Gorilla in Our Midst

Imagine that you are asked to watch a short recording of a basketball match; one team is wearing black and the other is wearing white. Your task is to count the number of passes made by the team in white as the ball is passed, between them, back and forth. Just like most people, I'm pretty sure you would have little difficulty in counting these; an easy enough task for most people. Now, imagine while you are doing this a man dressed in a gorilla costume walks slowly onto the basketball court. Having rubbed shoulders with several of the players, he turns towards you and beats his hands off his chest, before turning around and walking slowly off the court. Would you have any trouble spotting that gorilla? I can almost hear your laughter. Of course you wouldn't! That's what I thought too!

But when this research was carried out by eminent psychologists, Simons and Chabris, at Harvard University, they found that over fifty per cent of people who watched the recording did not spot the large hairy gorilla in their midst. When asked if they had seen anything odd or unusual during the video, more than half of the study participants had failed to see anyone apart from the players. They were so focused on counting the passes that they did not notice what was right under their noses. In fact, when the study participants were shown the recording again for a second time, many believed it had been altered or doctored in some way. They were adamant that the gorilla wasn't present when they watched the recording the first time. This interesting experiment highlights a concept known as 'perceptual blindness'. It suggests that our attention is similar to a filter system that allows only a certain amount of information to hit our conscious awareness at any one time. There is a limit to how much you can concentrate on and if your attention is at overload, it is entirely possible to miss things that are right in front of you – including big hairy gorillas! Of course basketball experts had no problem in spotting the gorilla: their expertise and passion for basketball meant they had the spare capacity for other tasks besides simply counting the passes.

The bottom line is that everyone has their blind spots. You may believe that you can see everything around you until you learn that owls can see in the dark and bees make out patterns written in ultraviolet light on flowers. You see the world not as it is, but as a representational map of who you are. As you change on the inside, so too does your map and outer reality change. Plutarch, the philosopher, put it well when he wrote that your inner journey determines your outer reality. There is no cure for perceptual blindness; however, being aware of its possibility is a good place to start. Heightened self-awareness will also make you more in tune with your own thoughts and how you see your environment. Develop your own internal 'sensometer' – not only to listen but to hear, not only to see but to really observe. Develop an attitude of curiosity, trusting and innocence and watch as your awareness and inner security deepens and develops.

Discovering Your Inner Compass

Just as you work out, take aerobic exercise or do some weight training to strengthen your muscles (and I believe exercise is the greatest pill of all!), you should consider your psychological fitness in much the same way. It's something else you have to work on, to build and develop. The Dalai Lama speaks about the Tibetan word *Sem* which means literally training the mind but has a more inclusive meaning of heart and mind, feeling and intellect, psyche or spirit.

Your brain is not a solid wooden structure with fixed capability; on the contrary, it's rather soft and doughy and can be stretched and strengthened just like a muscle. This is called neuroplasticity: the inbuilt capacity of the brain to change and evolve, not just when you are a child or teenager, but throughout your lifetime. This means that you can continue to develop your brain, just like you can keep on strengthening your muscles. Your brain can rewire in response to new inputs, enabling you to realise more of your potential happiness.

The fundamental importance of a good diet to optimal physical health is beyond repute – 'you are what you eat.' Similarly, the quality of your thinking, also known as your mental diet, is one of the most important components of psychological fitness. You tend to attract into your life the dominant thoughts you have inside your brain; in essence, it all starts with your thinking. Every thought you have is an opportunity to redefine your thinking, to reshape your beliefs, reframe your future life story minute by minute, hour by hour, day by day in the hidden recesses of your mind.

Every thought can influence the choices you make throughout your day, even though you are consciously unaware of most of them. Every thought can influence your character and move you closer to or further from the person you want to become. Every thought counts! You can build thoughts of success or failure, molehills or mountains, positivity or negativity. Your thoughts become the foundation of your psychological fitness – it's up to you!

Henry David Thoreau, the American philosopher, wrote

that just as 'a single footstep will not make a path on the earth, so a single thought will not make a pathway in the mind. To make a deep physical path, we walk again and again. To make a deep mental path, we must think over and over the kind of thoughts we wish to dominate our lives.' Your thoughts can have a powerful impact on your emotions (the Poison and Happy Dwarfs), as well as shaping your attitudes and your behaviour. At the end of the day you are who you think you are.

In many parts of the East, where Hinduism or Buddhism are practised, people start their day with the following prayer:

Who is it that is acting?
Who is it that is willing?
Who is it that is thinking?
Who am I?

Self-awareness helps you to better understand this 'I', the inner voice of conscience and responsibility, and the importance of connecting with and acting through it. By bringing a real sense of authenticity to your actions, self-awareness allows you to know more clearly what you value, and – guided by those values or inner compass – enables you to act with more integrity.

Self-awareness is simply seeing things as they are and approaching everything as if you were seeing them for the first time. The key to self-awareness is waking up and paying attention, becoming more attuned to those thoughts that produce the results you have right now in your life. This allows you to become more open and accepting of life's situations as they are, freeing up vital energy. The best way to prepare for the future is to be fully self-aware in the present moment. Self-awareness helps you to master your attention and your intentions because what you pay attention to grows in influence in your mind.

Self-awareness is being aware of what is happening right now in the moment rather than sleepwalking your way through your daily routines. By recognising your thoughts, emotions and behaviours as they occur, you can develop a better level of self-understanding and psychological insight. It means being able to step outside of yourself and observe yourself in action – dispassionately and without emotion. By opening your eyes to who you truly are, self-awareness can set you free from the regrets of the past or the worries and anxieties about the future, allowing you to simply be in the present moment.

Self-awareness helps you to recognise, celebrate and nurture your strengths as well as identify your weaknesses. It can help you to see yourself in a positive but realistic light, to attain perspective and to be more reflective and accepting of yourself as a genuine but fallible and imperfect human being.

Healthy humility makes you more sensitive to the needs of others. Accepting that you could be wrong and others right promotes a healthy level of self-criticism. Self-awareness can help you to cultivate this sense of healthy humility, opening up the possibility of learning from the experiences, strengths and achievements of others.

Self-awareness involves separating what someone says or does from your reaction to or judgement about it. Self-awareness helps you to realise that you have the power to *choose* how you respond. In this way, self-awareness helps you to take personal responsibility for your actions, to understand the consequences of those actions and to follow through on your commitments.

Think Thyroid! The thyroid gland is a small gland at the front of the neck that makes thyroid hormone, which, like the oil in the engine of the car, helps to keep the body ticking over. Sometimes, the thyroid gland can slow down and become underactive: too little thyroid hormone resulting in symptoms like tiredness, weight gain and cold intolerance. Fortunately, this condition is normally easily diagnosed by a blood test and is treated by replacing the vital hormone.

These very same principles can be applied to your negative thoughts which are estimated by psychologists to account for the vast majority of the 50,000 thoughts you have each day. That's a lot of negative thoughts! Needless negativity can become a self-handicapping scourge which can nudge you further and further from your goals and from the person you want to become. Negative thoughts can grab your attention and, as they persist, grow to become increasingly significant in your own mind, resulting in the poison dwarfs and negative actions in your life. Whatever you focus on, you are going to experience; if you have an urge to go negative, you are not going to produce anything positive. If you do not have enough happy dwarfs to counteract the poison dwarfs, then you can dip into a downward spiral.

You cannot get rid of a negative thought by simply blocking it out. You have to replace it with a more positive thought instead. This means you can swap a negative thought for a positive thought, an average thought for an amazingly brilliant thought. Replace those poison dwarfs; substitute them, get them off the stage. Replace thoughts of fear with thoughts of security; envy with thoughts of gratitude; anger with thoughts of peacefulness; anxiety with thoughts of calm; guilt with thoughts of contentment; hate with thoughts of love; sadness with thoughts of joy. When you have thoughts of doubt, replace them with thoughts of boldness; despair with thoughts of hope; discontent with thoughts of appreciation. Starve the fears, the doubts and insecurities in your life by no longer feeding them with the focus of your attention.

So, the more your mind focuses on positive aspects of your relationships, the stronger they become. The more you focus on your spiritual health, the greater your spiritual convictions become. By emphasising the more positive aspects of your job and career, you will feel more fulfilled at work.

The next time you experience a persistent negative thought, press the pause button in your brain. Reflect before you respond. Ask yourself; what are the consequences of this negative thought I am choosing to focus on? Will this thought that I am choosing to focus on right now bring happiness and contentment to me and to those around me? What is the most appropriate and positive response I can give?

Heightened self-awareness allows you to be the leader in your own life, a pilot rather than the passenger, turning your stumbling blocks into stepping stones of opportunity. Ultimately, this commitment to self-leadership opens up the possibility of transformational change, with the freedom to fulfil your creative potential and expand your happiness.

The Power of the Journal

Keeping a journal can be one of the best ways to improve your health and happiness by allowing you to closely monitor your thinking, emotions and behaviour. The Greek philosophers used their journals (called *hupomnemata*) at the end of each day to describe their day in terms of what went well and what could have gone better. One of the best exponents of the journal was the Roman Emperor, Marcus Aurelius, who, 2,000 years ago, wrote *Meditations* (the literal translation is 'thoughts to myself') as a reflective journal to challenge his attitude to irrational thoughts and to consider wiser responses.

Your journal provides a safe place to ask yourself thought-provoking and challenging questions and to contemplate the answers. It empowers you to wake up, to become more self-aware, to learn and grow. Keeping a journal helps you to stop being defensive about your situation in life – to stop resisting and become more accepting of people and situations as they truly are. It's an opportunity to figure out how to develop yourself in a better way, to set and work towards your goals and to become a better person.

Socrates, the Greek philosopher and father of medicine, wrote that one of the keys to an enlightened life is to 'know thyself'; that the unexamined life is not worth living. Writing your thoughts and feelings in your journal is a great way to get to know yourself better; the very process of writing will help you to build massive amounts of self-awareness. You will increase your understanding of those things that are most important to you and become much more focused, purposeful and intentional with your thoughts. This heightened awareness allows you to focus on what is and what isn't working in your life, allowing you to face the truth of your life for what it really is. It helps to understand better where you are right now in your life, who you are and who you are becoming. Better insight will give you the crystal-clear clarity needed to begin to change or improve those things that need to change or improve.

Recording your daily insights allows you to re-evaluate your experiences and so-called failures as the learning experiences they really are and offer real opportunities to grow. Keeping a journal strengthens self-discipline and a strong sense of personal commitment.

When you connect your brain through your hand to your journal and write down those thoughts, feelings and goals that are important to you, they become imprinted and impressed on your mind. This focus will allow your mind to give these written thoughts much more importance and significance than the many thousands of other thoughts that are passing through each day and to make the inner changes that can lead to external positive changes in your life. If you want to change your outer reality your thinking has to change first. All meaningful and lasting change comes from the inside.

Writing in your journal allows you to better recognise your strengths. It can also help your mind to attract the people, resources, ideas, information and wisdom that will support you in achieving your goals. Using your journal to work towards and sometimes achieve your written goals, no matter how small, can give a tremendous feeling of achievement.

Protecting your thinking is vital for your well-being. One of the great things about keeping a journal is that it allows you to monitor your thoughts closely. As you become more self-aware, it wakes you up to their impact in your life and provides you with the platform to improve: to focus on progress, not perfection. Enjoy the journey of this transformative process as you get to know and understand yourself better and at the same time make lasting improvements in your life. As you record and reflect your daily progress you can be inspired by life's little victories, those small one per cent wins that, over time, can transform your life. Decision-making can become better, more objective and less emotive by taking the time to write about the pros and cons of a certain course of action in your journal.

If you are like most people, then the vast majority of your thoughts tend to be the same thoughts you had yesterday and the day before. Thinking those same thoughts and beliefs repeatedly reinforces those brain pathways that got you to where you are today. There's a bit of chicken and egg here; negative thoughts create poison dwarfs, leading to actions and behaviours that reinforce those negative thoughts even more. The bottom line is that you can create a loop of reinforcing behaviour which can keep you stuck in a downward negative spiral.

Writing in your journal allows you to catch negative thoughts and beliefs as they arise; to write them down before they turn into poison dwarfs. This can be a very productive way of processing any frustrations you might be experiencing and can enable you to challenge and reappraise your thinking. Consider setting aside a specific time in your journal during the week when you can deal with your negative issues, worries or concerns. Doing negativity by appointment only allows you to reduce the impact of needless negativity in your day-to-day life.

You can use your journal to rethink the past and to imagine the future by putting a frame around something that enables you to see it from a different perspective. Recalling a negative experience in your life and writing about it in your journal can be a very healthy way to deal with that experience. It allows you to create a new narrative through the lens of improved understanding and find a sense of meaning and resolution.

Thinking outside the box involves letting go of your assumptions and opening your mind to new possibilities, becoming more creative and broad-minded in your outlook. One of the key benefits of your journal is being able to use every experience you have as an opportunity to learn something useful and make improvements, even if the improvement is only an improved understanding of yourself, your relationship or your situation.

Your thoughts can determine your reality; how you think determines how you act and how you act determines how other people react to you. The only person that can create the results you produce in your life is yourself; it starts with you! Negative thinking patterns consume valuable mental energy; while they might give you a temporary emotional tonic, any boost tends to be short-lived. If you allow yourself to be influenced by those people who will try and keep you small, they'll tell you all the reasons why something can't be done, why you are crazy to even attempt to improve yourself. You may be programmed by your fears, doubts or insecurities, by the flood of bad news in the negative headlines that will take you further and further from the person you want to become.

By triggering the poison dwarfs, negative thinking patterns can keep you stuck in an emotional straitjacket, inhibiting you from growing as a person. By keeping a journal of your own thoughts and dwarfs, you can become much more aware of your thinking style over time, catch any negative thinking patterns as they arise and challenge their authenticity.

As a medical doctor I am used to diagnosing people with different forms of -itis because in medicine, the word -itis commonly means inflammation or infection of a certain part of the body. For example, infection of the white part of your eye may be called conjunctivitis; infection of the tonsils is called tonsillitis and acute abdominal pain may be due to, among other things, acute appendicitis or diverticulitis. Similarly, I have experienced people suffering from various forms of -itis of their thinking which has led me to consider some of the following toxic thinking patterns; see if any of them relate to you or people in your life!

Worryitis

Every minute spent worrying about the way things were or are is a minute taken from the way things can be. With a tendency to worry excessively, you can over-generalise, interpret your feelings as facts, and exaggerate the negative consequences. So, for example, you don't succeed at a job interview and you believe you will never get a job again.

'Doomsday-scenario' thinking is a form of worryitis where you imagine all the bad things that might happen at some notional time in the future. By mentally engaging with what is stressing you, you choose to live by the 'what if' of some hypothetical future rather than the 'what is' of the present moment. 'What if I don't pass the exam? What if I can't pay the mortgage? What if I don't make the team?' This is closely related to 'assumption' thinking where you assume you know the outcome of a situation ahead of time, ignoring a broad range of evidence and then blowing out of all proportion a particular aspect of an event. You assume and predict the worst-case scenario without a shred of evidence in the world except that you 'know.' You may have 'why me' thinking: a form of worryitis that involves taking things on board in an inappropriate and emotionally loaded way. With a tendency to relate all kinds of external events back to yourself, a pattern of focusing endlessly and repetitively on negative thoughts and feelings may develop, as well as their potential causes and consequences. You become obsessed with 'why did he say that?', 'why did he do that?', and 'what am I doing wrong?' All-or-nothing thinking is a type of worryitis characterised by the use of extreme words like always or never; there is no middle ground, everything is either right or wrong. At the root of perfectionism, this type of thinking is a guaranteed journey to misery and pessimism. (Remember the philosopher Voltaire who wrote not to let the perfect be the enemy of the good!)

Entitleitis

This is the 'myth of entitlement', the culture of ingratitude and thanklessness so prevalent today. These are the people who feel that the world owes them, that the world needs to change and recognise their special qualities. However they do not believe they need to do anything about it. Many people can suffer from this myth, that somehow you simply deserve to have health, wealth and happiness without any effort on your part. That expecting special treatment or being exempt from following the rules is your entitlement. That all you have to do is show up and it's all yours; that you don't have to do anything to nurture your health, earn your wealth or cultivate your happiness. They want to reap but not sow. They want it all, right now!

Entitleitis can encourage you to become a volunteer victim, overreacting to minor things, blowing them out of proportion while often remaining indifferent to those really important things in life. This is the belief that when you fail or things don't work out as planned, it's always someone else's fault, triggering frustration, resentment or poison dwarf type anger. And if you feel unhappy that it's because you are a victim of someone or something else. Entitleitis can breed negative know-all thinking; knowing all the reasons to be negative, becoming an expert at remembering you are entitled to your outbursts of negative emotion, so you hold on to your negativity and wallow in it. You have an argument and you feel entitled to hold on to your anger, knowing you are right, becoming an advocate for your own negativity. This consumes so much negative energy, distracting you from your potential to sort out the initial problem. The best antidote to entitleitis is a healthy dose of humility.

'Control-freak' thinking is a form of entitleitis, where you believe you are entitled to control everything in order to feel happy or safe in the world, a recipe for certain disappointment and guilt when things do not go as planned. Real life is what happens while you are busy making plans; many people can disappoint if you allow them to. The rollercoaster of life is the reality that many people experience; ultimately the only person that you can change in this world is yourself.

Compareitis

Comparing yourself to others that are more successful, beautiful, or smarter than you is a sure way to trigger poison dwarfs like Envy. Instead, compare yourself to your future potential and work on the journey within. Of course you can also feel happier and more content by comparing yourself to people less fortunate than you and being grateful for all you have. It's all about choosing your comparisons carefully.

'If only' thinking is a form of compareitis where the focus is on the faraway hills, which always appear greener but in truth rarely are. This type of thinking diminishes and detracts from the choices you have made, leading to dissatisfaction and a sense of regret. While it is invaluable to learn from your mistakes, not letting go of regret can be unproductive, leading to rumination and pessimism. Being happier and more present is a journey, not a destination. Drifting off, being distracted and not paying attention can cause unhappiness. One of the best ways to break a positive mood is to ask why it can't always be like this; you will quickly remind yourself of all the reasons why. You may feel that 'if only' this or that was different, then your life would be so much better.

In life you have your own race to run so you should ensure that's the race you do run. There is no point in trying to run somebody else's race for them. Everyone has their own unique talents and potential. There is nothing noble in being superior to others; true nobility lies in being superior to your former self.

Me-itis

Mirror, mirror, on the wall, who is the fairest of them all? 'Me-itis' is also known as the disease of 'me'. 'Me-itis' is the illusion of self-sufficiency. Some of the symptoms are a swelled head, an overinflated ego and opinion of yourself, the desire for constant approval and applause and the inability and unwillingness to recognise your own vulnerability.

You can become obsessed with what others think of you and spend valuable time and energy trying to live up to that image, leading to middle-aged spread of your brain as you become increasingly self-satisfied, smug and more resistant to change. 'Me-itis' can make you complacent and lull you into a false sense of security with a constant need for attention and admiration.

Success can foster 'Me-itis.' It can mislead you into thinking you are the success, forgetting about the discipline, hard work and support from others that got you there. 'Me-itis' can result in loss of focus and reduce your willingness to take risks. Instead, you stay in cruise control, protecting what you have, believing that you don't have to support others. You can lose your drive to succeed and stop doing the things that made you successful in the first place. For lots of successful businesses and organisations, this can be the straw that breaks the camel's back.

Excusitis

You don't get a promotion at work, your relationship fails, or you don't make the team. No matter what happens, you have an excuse. Blame and complain about your childhood, your parents, or your lack of educational opportunities. Blame everyone and everything except the one person with the power to make a difference – *you*! It's so easy to blame everyone else when you don't achieve the results you desire in your life; to believe that the problem is out there somewhere, but nothing to do with you.

'Must-do' thinking is a form of excusitis; a classic sign of the life that is off track and rudderless, just like a leaf blowing in the wind. You have long lists of 'must-dos' but no goals or concrete action plan to deliver on them. 'Must-do' thinking can demoralise and disappoint when you don't deliver on all your 'must-do's.'

Being responsible means no more 'poor me syndrome', 'what ifs', or 'if onlys.' 'Being 100 per cent responsible means understanding that how you feel about everything in your life is down to you: only you can change how you feel and respond in any given situation. The truth is that to achieve major success in life you have to start to take 100 per cent responsibility – completely and unequivocally – for all of your actions. This requires the courage to be authentic and self-aware enough to take complete ownership of your own life.

If you think like a volunteer victim, you won't recognise your blind spots or foster any sense of appreciation for the gifts life has to offer you. Everything you make excuses about, blame someone else for and complain about is something that you can change if you choose to do so. Stop self-defeating behaviour or self-destructive habits; stop giving attention to negative noise or idle gossip. No more distractions, no more excuses! Empower yourself to dream bigger, to confidently embrace your goals, and to exorcise the excuses that have kept you stuck.

Thinking styles

Remember you can choose to excuse your negative thinking. You can let yourself off the hook, wallow in self-created sympathy and justify the reality you have created. Use your journal to rationally re-evaluate those thoughts that have the potential to create inner turbulence in your mind and put you on a downward spiral. Replace these thoughts with something more creative and meaningful and build your sense of realistic optimism.

Choosing to focus on what's going well and why can be so beneficial for your psychological well-being. The habit of simply writing down three things that went well each day and why in your journal can lead to increased happiness and fewer depressive symptoms. This can be effective at any time, but particularly first thing in the morning or last thing at night. As you express what you think and feel, you get to know yourself better and gain new insights: clarity which can lead to more objective decisions and better results in your life. Heightened self-awareness helps you to recognise patterns of thinking or behaviour that you may have difficulty letting go of otherwise.

By becoming more reflective, you can really strengthen your psychological fitness. The word 'attention' comes from the Latin for 'reach toward'. What you give your attention to really does matter! Why not give yourself a few minutes each day to write in your journal? The courage to do this can set you free to improve your health, transform your life and expand your happiness.

The Power of Belief

Beliefs are the internal rules that you live your life by. These rules may be energising and empowering, enabling you to live by your values. Beliefs can determine whether you work towards your goals, attain your potential and become the person you are capable of becoming. Simple belief can transform your life.

In early 1944, during World War Two, Henry Beecher, a young doctor from Harvard, was treating injured American soldiers in a makeshift field hospital in Anzio, Northern Italy. With many hundreds of wounded soldiers to deal with, his supply of pain-killing morphine soon ran out. In desperation, Beecher administered a salt water injection to a soldier with gaping wounds who lay awaiting his operation. Beecher found that the soldier, thinking he'd been injected with morphine, was comforted by the salt water, and was subsequently able to tolerate the trauma of the operation itself.

After the war Henry Beecher returned to Harvard and wrote about this 'placebo effect' – the impact that your own beliefs can have on your response to medical treatment. Today the placebo effect (Latin 'I shall please') is recognised to be a significant element in response to prescribed medication. It is the belief that a certain treatment will work, perhaps because of variables from the colour of the tablet to the reputation of the doctor prescribing it, but also because of each person's inbuilt health belief system.

The nocebo (Latin for 'I will harm') or reverse placebo effect is even more remarkable. This is where something that should be completely ineffective causes symptoms of ill health. These placebo and nocebo effects highlight how integral your mind sight and belief systems are to your reaction and response to medical treatment.

The placebo effect in action at the workplace was tested using the cleaning staff of seven hotels. Half of the employees were told how much exercise they were already getting each day at work and benefitting from as part of their normal work duties. For example it was highlighted how many steps were taken during their working day and how that equated to calories burned, how many calories were expended cleaning a bathroom or a bedroom, etc. The other half of the employees weren't told anything. Several weeks later, the authors of the experiment, Harvard Professor Ellen Langer and Ali Crum from Yale University, found that those employees conditioned to see their work as a workout lost weight and also dropped their cholesterol levels! These people had neither worked harder, nor taken any more exercise than the control group – it was just that their mind sight was different. They saw their work in a new light, in terms of its health-enhancing benefits. And these new insights produced tangible improvements in their health, bringing a new meaning to the term workout at work!

Time Travel

Ellen Langer, the brilliant Harvard-based psychologist, in 1979 designed a fascinating week-long experiment on a group of seventy-five-year-old men. They were taken to a retreat centre for a week, their only prior instruction being to bring with them no books, magazines or any material dated later than 1959 (twenty years earlier). On arrival the men were told that, for the following seven days, they had to pretend it was the year 1959, when these men were aged fifty-five years (twenty years younger). The environment they stayed in was simulated to resemble 1959 – in other words the newspapers, magazines and television programmes shown were all from that time.

Before the retreat started, the men were tested on many attributes presumed to deteriorate with age. These included physical strength, perception, posture, cognition and short-term memory. A week later, when the retreat ended, the men were retested. The results were remarkable. Most of the men had made significant improvements in terms of improved posture and flexibility, with even much-improved hand strength. Average eyesight and memory had improved almost ten per cent. And their physical appearance had changed as well. Photographs of each person, taken before and after the retreat, and independently assessed, found that the men looked, on average, at least three years younger after the week-long retreat.

Gandhi, the Indian statesman, had put it very well when he said: 'Your thoughts become your beliefs; your beliefs your words; your words your actions; your actions your habits; your habits your character and your character your destiny.' What you think about and choose to believe is closely connected to who you are and who you become. If you want to really see what a person believes deep down, don't listen to what they say, look at what they do. Your behaviour broadcasts your beliefs and your actions speak louder than your words.

Beliefs are important building blocks in the foundation of your psychological fitness. Your brain is like a sophisticated computer and may well be running programs that were learned and written before you even started school. Some of your beliefs may be questionable, keeping your thinking small, obstructing your path, blocking your progress. These limiting beliefs often come from your childhood and the negative messages received from your 'imperfect' parents and family network. Their limiting beliefs, riddled with negativity and insecurity (which they in turn may have learned from their family and their family before them) can be passed on to you like a baton in a relay race, and you may carry these with you for the rest of your life, not forgetting of course to pass them on at every opportunity. Here are some typical limiting beliefs: 'They will never pick me so it is not worth trying; I don't have enough time for exercise; I am too old to develop a new career.' Many people believe that problems in their lives are caused by external circumstances, by other people, by things they can't change or control. That very belief is part of the problem. In many respects you may be playing out the subconscious programming you received as a young child when you heard: 'Stop doing that; watch your place; don't get too big for your boots; don't get a swelled head.'

The problem with having limiting beliefs is that your fears, doubts and insecurities can become deeply ingrained with the result you may believe that you can't change. Furthermore they often act as an invisible straitjacket, keeping you stuck and producing self-handicapping and self-destructive behaviours that restrict the possibilities for your life.

Believing in yourself is a choice and you can choose your beliefs. Every belief you have has the potential to become a self-fulfilling prophecy. If you want to change and improve some aspect of your life then consider changing your beliefs. Believe in your inner resources and in the rich possibilities that your life can offer you. Believe in your potential to take daily steps to become the person you want to become, transform your life and turn your dreams into reality. Believe in the fundamental goodness of humanity, in the connectedness of all human beings and in the possibility of expanding your happiness. Believe in the power and possibility of belief itself!

Use your journal to explore your beliefs. Do you have any limiting beliefs that may be holding you back? Are they all valid and worthy of being kept or are there better alternatives?

The Power of Self-image

Your self-image is your own picture of yourself as a human being, a combination of your awareness and self-belief. It is your unique combination of thoughts, beliefs, emotions and memories, all bundled together to form the image you have of yourself. Self-image regulates your behaviour just like cruise control regulates the speed of your car on the motorway. Your self-image is the subconscious way in which you act out your life and you will never exceed the self-image you have of yourself. Your life can become a self-fulfilling prophecy with the results you expect in your life becoming the results that you see. It's often said that the most important opinion you have is the one you have of yourself, and the most significant things you say all day are those things you say to yourself.

Another way of considering your self-image is to think of it as your inner mirror whose reflection will determine how you use your time, knowledge and resources. If you can upgrade your thinking and reframe your beliefs, then you can change your self-image. The key is to decide on the kind of person you wish to become and act accordingly. As a result, your self-image can become a reflection of your behaviour and of your values.

Self-esteem, or inner sense of security, is about feeling worthy, and deserving of the success and many blessings in life that you have already received. It is based on your inner core as a human being and is completely detached from anything external including material goods, achievements, etc. The unconditional love that children receive from their parents as youngsters is one of the best ways to build self-esteem which can become the foundation stone for later success in life. Self-esteem is an important quality that is tied to happiness and inner contentment.

Use your journal to explore the reality of your self-image and how valid it really is. So many people never challenge the image they have of themselves and, as a result, fail to achieve more of their potential in life. Your self-image can give you lots of excuses and all the reasons in the world why you shouldn't improve and why you should stay just as you are.

Be the Change

Self-development is the commitment you make to yourself each and every day to learn something new or to improve in some way, no matter how small that may be. When I talk about self-development I mean understanding the power of learning and of effort; appreciating the power of words and the potential for distraction to undermine your efforts; the power of discipline, forgiveness and letting go. Benjamin Franklin once wrote that if a man empties his purse into his head, no one can take it away from him; an investment in knowledge always pays the best interest.

The Power of Learning

I believe passionately in the potential of education to improve your health, expand your happiness and transform your life. Real education is about developing and cultivating your mind: learning new things that upgrade your thinking by creating new connections and pathways in the brain and stimulating changes in brain chemistry that allow you to feel more energised. Education can protect you from depression, build your psychological fitness and give you the keys to inner freedom; it can be an astonishing source of lasting happiness and inner contentment.

One of the best ways to learn new things and develop your

mind is through reading. I believe in the benefit of reading magazines or journals that feed your mind, that stretch and challenge your thinking. Reading can provide both present benefit in terms of your enjoyment of the experience of learning as well as future benefit in terms of your personal and professional growth. Read the great biographies: inspiring books that encourage you to live and give in exceptional ways, that raise interesting questions and help you to grow in wisdom. Reading pays off: if you make the commitment to read at least a book a week, review what you have read and apply at least one thing you learn from each book into your life, you will be well on the road to mastery. One book a week adds up to fifty-two books a year, or 520 books in ten years. In twenty years more than 1,000 books, enough to put you into the top one per cent of experts in your chosen field. I believe that one of the most important aspects of self-development is this lifelong commitment to keep learning and improving. The pursuit of knowledge is a journey without a destination; the challenge is to stay on the path to wisdom and personal transformation. As you continue to work on your self-development, your self-esteem and inner confidence will soar.

The Power of Effort

Everyone can become an expert or achieve excellence in what they do. Moreover, it has surprisingly little to do with talent and much more to do with drive and determination! In *Bounce: The myth of talent and the power of practice*, author Matthew Syed demonstrates eloquently how in order to achieve mastery in any complex task, from sport to chess to academia, you need at least 10,000 hours of expert practice (which equates to about ten years of your life). This deliberate and purposeful practice is needed to get you out of your comfort zone, to stretch yourself beyond the bounds of your capabilities and challenge you to work on those things you currently don't do well. This can transform you into the expert you want to become. The paradox of excellence is that progress requires you to fall short and fail often on the journey to success. By embracing so-called failure as a necessary friend on this path to personal transformation, you learn more about yourself, the learning curve becomes exponential and your knowledge, skills and performance are magnified. By focusing on the journey of continuous improvement, small daily improvements over time can lead to truly amazing results in your life.

The Power of Words

There is an old Sufi saying: before you speak, let your words pass through three gates:

At the first gate, ask yourself: 'Is it true?'
At the second gate, ask yourself: 'Is it necessary?'
At the third gate, ask yourself: 'Is it kind?'

According to the *Rigveda*, widely considered to be the world's oldest spiritual text, all sounds have vibrational energy attached to them. And when you hear these triggers, you may experience a certain emotion and respond in a certain way. The words you use in your everyday language to yourself and others can have a major impact on how you feel. This is because your words have meaning and power; what you choose to say about someone is a reflection on you and your values. Your words reflect your beliefs, drive your actions and in turn create all of the results in your life. So have integrity of thought, word and action. Words you use today influence the world you experience tomorrow. Language you use today impacts on the life you lead tomorrow. The key is to speak from the heart in a manner that allows your words to be consistent with your values.

Wherever your words go your energy flows. So be true to your word, your work and your friends. Don't blame and complain, don't criticise or condemn. Consider being more positive and uplifting with your language. Not only will you feel better and your energy elevate but you will inspire those around you. Remember that the quality of the conversations you have in part determines the quality of your life. Be committed to having more positive conversations about things that really matter and watch your outlook on life improve.

Self-talk is a name for your inner conversation, the continuous dialogue and tape that is playing 24/7, with an endless commentary about life, your problems, and other people. So often it judges, blames and complains, telling you all the reasons why you can't achieve your goals, or make positive changes. Emerson, the American philosopher, wrote that you are what you think about all day long. What you tell yourself in your mind is the basis on which you determine your experience of reality. It can become so automatic and engrained that it forms the foundations of who you are.

Imagine if you could transform your negative self-talk into positive self-talk, turn your inner critic into your inner coach and prevent the self-handicapping scourge of needless negativity. The use of positive self-talk can help you make the internal change so necessary before you see external positive changes in your life. And your self-talk is already there as a powerful force in your life; it is not something you have to create. Self-talk can help determine your 'X factor' and the likelihood of the successful completion of a task or accomplishment of a goal. You see it isn't enough to simply plan and get ready; you need to take action and get started and positive self-talk can allow you to do just that.

Affirmations are strong positively worded statements that something is already so. They are an excellent way of transforming old negative self-talk with more positive thoughts and encouraging ideas. Use your journal to keep a scrapbook of affirmations, inspirational quotes or uplifting poems; they can give you a spiritual shot in the arm when you need them most.

Even a few minutes a day of reading and repeating positive affirmations in your journal can have a powerful impact on your psychological fitness and sense of well-being. There are so many types of affirmations to choose from. Here are a few of my favourites:

Small daily improvements over time, lead to amazing results.

I am an open channel of abundant, creative energy.

Perfect wisdom is in my heart.

The Power of Distraction

We live in a world of endless distraction. Ask yourself this question: is what you're doing each day contributing to your happiness? Does any of it clutter and complicate your life? Let's take television for example. Now TV can be a good servant but a very bad master. If you are organised enough to plan your TV schedule a week in advance, you can select those programmes of most interest to you and your family. Given that the average person may watch more than three hours of TV a day, this translates to forty-five days of non-stop TV watching per year and more than eleven years over a typical ninety-year lifespan. Do you really want to spend such a large part of your life watching other people living out their dreams while you are stagnating? There is never enough time to do everything but there is enough time to do the right things. Simply cutting out one hour of TV a day gives you an additional 365 hours a year (over nine additional forty-hour weeks); two more months to pursue your goals and work on your own self-development. Two more months of possibility; developing your mind and broadening your horizons.

If you eat junk food you may feel stodgy, tired and bloated. In the longer term, if you eat it regularly, you can become obese, diabetic and develop a whole range of other health-related complications. It is the same for your psychological fitness. If your mind is exposed to and fed enough negativity then, sooner or later, negative thoughts and actions are going to show up in your life. Negative noise is everywhere, the blaming and complaining, people arguing passionately in favour of their limitations. Listen to any conversation for a period of time and you will hear the negativity, the toxic chatter. Most of the time the news could be better called 'the bad news'. How often do you hear a good news story? Even the weather gets reported in negative terms: a sixty per cent chance of sunshine, reported instead as a forty per cent chance of rain. Recognise the power of the media and your environment to influence your mood: you may well become what you watch! And watch out who you become as a result. The more TV you watch, the more violent you tend to perceive the world around you. Watching violent and programmes can also desensitise you to violence, increase your chances of becoming violent, as well as diluting your capacity for empathy and kindness.

Experiments by social psychologist Albert Bandura using Bobo dolls in the 1960s, and described in his book *Self-Efficacy, the Exercise of Control,* found that children readily absorb and apply lessons from their environment: violence becomes a form of learned behaviour by watching and then imitating violent adults. Philip Zimbardo, author of *The Lucifer Effect: Understanding How Good People Turn Evil,* went even further. In his 'Stanford Prison Experiment', Zimbardo took twenty-four healthy male volunteers and split them into two-groups of twelve – one group were inmates and the other guards. A two-week experiment to monitor behaviour in a simulated prison environment had to be abandoned after only a few days as some of the wardens had become so sadistic that the inmates had emotional breakdowns!

Sometimes the impact of the media can be more subtle, influencing and recalibrating your view of what's normal from hero to size zero. As a result it can be easy to feel you don't measure up and young people, in particular, can be submerged by the poison dwarf called Shame.

In many respects your mind is like a soft sponge, soaking up all of its exposures. What happens when you squeeze a sponge? You can only reap what you sow: squeezing out only what was initially soaked up, these thoughts come out as actions and behaviours in your life. The challenge is to become more aware of all the different influences on your attention and thinking: you really do become your associations. Because of the mirroring effect, you can take on the attitudes, beliefs, daily habits, sometimes even the body language and mannerisms of those people you spend most time with.

Using your journal, carry out an audit of the negative noise you expose yourself to on a daily basis. Include the people you associate with, the language you hear and use, the television you watch, the newspapers you read. Can you cut back on some needless negativity in your life?

The Power of Discipline

In the 1960s, a now famous experiment was started by psychologist Walter Mischell at Stanford University. Marshmallows were put in front of young four-year-old children by their teacher with the instruction that the pupils could eat one marshmallow there and then. However, if they could resist eating for fifteen minutes while she left the room, their reward would be two marshmallows instead of one. Not surprisingly, only thirty per cent of the children were able to withstand the temptation and were rewarded with the two marshmallows (after all they were only aged four at the time!). Follow-up studies many years later revealed that those very same children who had resisted the marshmallow were more resilient, self-confident and self-reliant. They experienced better interpersonal relationships, embraced challenges better and performed much better on their academic test scores.

Self-control means being able to act in accordance with your own values, to make better emotional decisions, to control your impulses or the desire to 'act' in a particular way. This ability to withstand the heat in the kitchen, to resist temptation, and to delay gratification is one of the fundamentals of emotional intelligence. Understanding the difference between emotions and actions and the acceptability or otherwise of certain behaviour patterns underpins every sort of achievement and accomplishment in life. Characteristics of self-regulation include thoughtfulness, integrity and the ability, plain and simple, to say no.

Self-control is like a muscle: by exercising it, you build and strengthen it. Like any muscle, if overused, it can get fatigued. Build it by regular practice – stretching it (but not to breaking point) allows it to strengthen. The key here is self-discipline (the stickability factor); taking specific actions day in and day out to keep you moving in the direction of your goals. The opposite of self-control is self-indulgence: the desire for the quick fix, for instant gratification, bypassing the ingredients for long-term success namely discipline, effort and persistence.

The Power of Letting Go

Learning to let go keeps you more in the moment, supporting your own happiness and well-being. The Chinese philosopher Lin Yutang wrote about the psychological freedom and true peace of mind which comes from accepting the worst, with the realisation that there is nothing further to lose and the possibility of everything to gain. Look at your own thinking patterns and stop struggling, blaming or complaining: this is a waste of energy! Let go of any resentment you feel towards people who have hurt you in the past. Let go of 'having' and focus more on 'being' and 'valuing', opening your heart and mind to be more respectful and tolerant of the views of others. Understand that the only person you can change is yourself. Better to take responsibility for your own thoughts, feelings and actions rather than wasting energy trying to change someone else. Having brought you to the place you are today, the past has served its purpose. Staying stuck in the past precludes you from experiencing happiness right now, in the present. Be grateful for and learn from your past experiences but understand that the present moment is all you have. Attachment is based on insecurity and fear; developing a sense of non-attachment and learning to 'let go' of the past (which is the only thing that is known) can help you to overcome that poison dwarf called Fear. Instead embrace uncertainty as an essential, yet unknown, ingredient of your experiences. Let your past go so you can grow! If you feel mistreated or misunderstood by someone, you can become obsessed about getting an apology, an acknowledgement or admission that that person has wronged you. Your experience, your world, tells you that you are right, but so does theirs. Each with their own perspective, everyone sees the world as they are, not as it is. While there are situations or occasions in life where an apology may be indicated, better instead to take ownership of your emotional well-being by simply letting go of this need to be right! Let go of the worry and anxiety about the future, that illusion of control over future events. Let go of the need to impress others. Instead work on becoming the most real and authentic version of yourself that is possible. When you accept who you are and share yourself with others, you will radiate authenticity. People will appreciate how real and genuine you are and you will be seen for the wonderful person that you really are. When you choose to let go, you stop struggling, manipulating, trying so hard and simply be. Letting things be as they are can be wonderfully liberating. In Christianity, 'God's will be done.' In Buddhist philosophy, 'letting go of attachment.'

Letting Go of Stress

No discussion about psychological fitness would be complete without mentioning stress. Everyone has some stress in their daily life and stress, per se, doesn't actually do you any harm. In fact, some stress can be very good for you. It can help you perform better under pressure and motivate you to achieve excellence and elite performance; you wouldn't be able to get out of bed in the morning without some level of stress. Acute stress can, quite literally, save your life (the fight or flight response – remember the bear in the woods story!).

However, when stress turns to distress and begins to impact negatively on your health and well-being, that is when problems can arise. The issue is not enough balance or relief from stress (not enough of the happy dwarfs to counteract the poison dwarfs), rather than stress per se.

To protect yourself from the potentially very damaging effects of negative stress, it is important to have balance so you can be really resilient and bounce back. Excess negative stress can cause distress and put you on a downward spiral on the road towards despair, despondency and depression. You can develop a more pessimistic outlook, heightened negative self-talk, and negative thinking patterns like black-cloud thinking. Moodiness and short-fused irritability can dominate the landscape. Poor concentration, shortened attention span and impaired judgement can result in procrastination or neglect of responsibilities. Distress can result in people adopting more unhealthy coping strategies such as smoking, binge-drinking or comfort-eating – behaviours which can be self-defeating in terms of your happiness, health and well-being. Self-doubt, or feeling overwhelmed with life, can lower self-esteem and predispose to alcohol or other substance abuse (which in themselves can aggravate feelings of distress).

Excessive stress can be toxic and damaging for your professional and personal relationships, pushing people away and resulting in feelings of isolation and disconnection from others. This can lead to a sense of loneliness and decreased contact with family and friends or work colleagues. Rewiring of your brain from chronic distress can make you more susceptible to the poison dwarfs like Fear, Anger and Guilt, precipitating panic attacks, anxiety and prolonged feelings of sadness with a destructive trail in their wake. These guys can cause real emotional havoc when it comes to your emotional well-being, leaving you feeling burnt out, empty on the inside, devoid of meaning.

Stress causes the release of hormones including adrenaline, noradrenaline and cortisol which surge through the body and can weaken the immune system, making you more vulnerable to viral infections like colds and flu when you are run down and delaying the healing response.

With chronic long-term distress, weakening of the immune system can cause wear and tear throughout the various organs in the body. Chronic sustained stress can even cause wear and tear on the brain itself, which can affect memory and can also speed up the ageing process. Many people no longer ask which illnesses are related to stress; rather how much of every illness is induced by negative stress.

The key to destress is to achieve more balance in your life. Have you heard of the yin and the yang: balance and counterbalance, the cycle of peak performance followed by rest, recharge and strategic renewal? Have the right balance (at least 3:1) of happy to poison dwarfs; be more playful, nurture your inner child. Focus on your strengths. Instead of procrastination and the pursuit of perfection, focus on progress and clarify what is really important for you. By making time for the truly important things in your life, you can manage time wisely rather than allowing your time to manage you. Maintain perspective, don't turn your molehills into mountains – if little things frustrate you, then big things will destroy you. Don't argue for your limitations, reduce negative self-talk and learn to live more in the moment. Meditate regularly; empty your mind and enjoy the benefits that ensue. Spend time with nature: it nourishes your mind and nurtures your soul.

The Power of Forgiveness

Learning to forgive those people who have hurt you can be a very powerful way to expand your happiness. It is also important to forgive yourself; everyone makes mistakes in life, the important thing is to acknowledge and learn from them and then move on. Mark Twain once wrote that 'forgiveness is the fragrance that the violet sheds on the heel that has crushed it.' I believe forgiveness should be a key component of your psychological fitness; in addition, forgiveness fosters friendship and feeling closer to others, promotes flourishing and can set you free.

I have learned that real self-forgiveness is more than lip service: it's a journey within to a place deep in your heart. A place that speaks to you from your core and allows you to be truly authentic. A place that forgives you for being far from perfect in an imperfect world, for finding it difficult to let go of old ways of thinking. And at the same time a place which allows you to embrace the freedom to accept yourself, warts and all, for who you are. Self-forgiveness has helped me to understand that pressing the pause button is all part of the journey of exploration, a journey which has allowed me to figure out who I am and to understand that my real purpose in life is to be a more effective resource in supporting others in improving their lives. Understanding clearly for the first time that being a better resource to myself is the starting point of that journey and not the finish line.

Forgiveness is an ongoing process and journey, not an end point in itself. There are always some people out there who are going to be nasty, vindictive and insensitive; that's just the way life is. Remember the Sioux Indian prayer: 'Don't judge a man until you have walked Two Moons in his moccasins.' Instead of hating enemies, be thankful that life has not made you what they are; instead of heaping revenge or condemnation upon your enemies, give them your understanding, sympathy, and forgiveness. Learn to practise more self-acceptance of the people, places and situations in your life as they are right now; write about this in your journal. I'm reminded of the beautiful words in the Serenity Prayer, attributed to the American theologian, Neibuhr:

'God, grant me the serenity to accept the things I cannot change;

The courage to change the things I can;

And the wisdom to know the difference.'

The Parable of the Chinese Bamboo Tree

I recall reading a Chinese proverb that the best time to plant a tree was twenty years ago and the second best time is now! There is something truly majestic about trees and Ireland has such a wide variety to admire and enjoy. But my favourite tree, the Chinese bamboo tree, doesn't even grow in Ireland. This tree grows in Southwest Asia and the reason I like it so much is because of what it represents. Imagine taking a Chinese bamboo tree seed and planting it in a favourable aspect of your garden. You feed it, water it, cultivate the soil and weed the area around it carefully for a whole year. Apart from a tiny sprout, nothing happens, but you don't give up or dig up the seed and plant it somewhere else. You keep going. In years two, three and four, you continue to feed and water the seed but still nothing happens. You're discouraged but you don't give up. Then sometime in year five, the Chinese bamboo tree starts to grow and in the space of just five weeks, grows between eighty and ninety feet tall!

The question is, did the bamboo tree grow ninety feet in five weeks or five years? The answer, of course, is five years! During the first four years, the Chinese bamboo tree *was* growing. The growth was invisible but underground; the tree was developing the extensive root structure and strong foundations to support its later upward growth.

The same principles of nurturing the Chinese bamboo tree seed apply to your goals, your belief systems and your life. It is so important to have belief: to build a strong foundation, to plan and persist, to persevere and be resilient. Remember the power of consistent effort and belief; to continue to do things right; to have belief that you can succeed. As long as you keep feeding and watering your dreams, there is every possibility they will eventually come to fruition. You must have faith in your own bamboo tree seeds whether they are to raise well-adjusted children, build your business or expand your happiness.

The challenge, of course, is the culture of instant gratification and sense of entitlement so prevalent nowadays; the lack of patience and demand for instant solutions to every complex problem or challenged relationship.

You may want to dig up your Chinese bamboo tree seed and plant it elsewhere, in more fertile ground, believing that faraway hills are always greener. There is also a tendency to compare yourself to others and get frustrated at their apparent progress compared to you. Just like other trees or shrubs in your garden you can be doing things right in life and nothing might happen. You have to be prepared to pay the price, to prepare the ground, to plant the seed and persevere. You can set your goals, work towards them and still nothing happens. Sometimes, when you are tantalisingly close to realising them, you may become discouraged and give up on your dreams and aspirations. *Don't!* In many respects, the Chinese bamboo tree is the metaphor for patience. Real life often works the same way: you can spend weeks, months, even years with seemingly little or no external progress and then things suddenly can start to take off.

The parable of the Chinese bamboo tree is also known as 'The Lucky Bamboo Tree'. In Chinese culture, especially in feng shui, it is believed to bring positive energy to the home and to establish the proper balance among the natural elements of earth, fire, metal, water and wood. In a similar vein, you can establish the principles of balance between the physical, psychological, relationship and emotional aspects of your health and happiness.

The bamboo tree grows tall and upright and is recognised as being resilient, tenacious and highly adaptable. The bamboo tree has a hollow centre, representing an open heart full of compassion, empathy and optimism while never arrogant or prejudiced. In Chinese culture the bamboo tree is a symbol of longevity while in India it is a symbol of friendship.

Are you committed to fine-tuning your psychological fitness? Are you forward thinking? Plant the Chinese bamboo tree seeds in your mind today that can bring the results you deserve in your life five years from now.

Part 2

My Charter for Action

Ten Commitments

to Expand Your Happiness

Ten Commitments
1. Gratitude
2. Kindness
3. Relationships
4. Goals
5. Time
6. Exercise
7. Realistic Optimism
8. Simplicity
9. Spirituality
10. Choice

Part 2 of this book explores my charter for action – how to integrate some of these happiness-expanding habits into your life. My ten commitments to support the possibility of you becoming happier include gratitude; kindness and compassion; building great relationships; goals that allow you to grow; making time for what matters; exercise; cultivating realistic optimism; embracing simplicity, spirituality and the courage to choose happiness. These commitments can all be learned and bedded down as happiness-building habits. What's more, perhaps the best way to deepen the learning is to teach these skills to your children, significant others, or someone in your life who matters to you.

A PRESCRIPTION FOR HAPPINESS

Here are my Ten Commitments to Expand Your Happiness:

- ꙮ The First Commitment: Gratitude – Dynamite for Your Well-being.

- ꙮ The Second Commitment: Kindness and Compassion – Live to Give.

- ꙮ The Third Commitment: Great Relationships – A Recipe for Real Contentment.

- ꙮ The Fourth Commitment: Goals – That Allow You to Grow.

- ꙮ The Fifth Commitment: Making Time – For What Matters.

- ꙮ The Sixth Commitment: Exercise – The Greatest Pill of All.

- ꙮ The Seventh Commitment: Realistic Optimism – Oxygen for Opportunity.

- ꙮ The Eighth Commitment: Simplicity – The Ultimate Sophistication.

- ꙮ The Ninth Commitment: Spirituality – The Purpose of Life is a Life of Purpose.

- ꙮ The Tenth Commitment: Courage – The Courage to Choose.

The First Commitment:

Gratitude – Dynamite for Your Well-being

Born, legally blind, to Norwegian parents in Minnesota in 1890, Borghild Dahl was completely blind in her right eye and her left eye was so covered with dense scars that she had to do all her seeing through a small opening in the left outer corner of the eye. But thanks to her extraordinary parents who clearly understood her obstacles but did not give in to them, she was enabled to live fully and productively. She was encouraged to read by holding a book up close to her face and by straining her one eye as hard as she could to the left. Borghild was expected to do household chores like everyone else. She described her steadfast determination to participate in every life experience. She went to mainstream school and

sat at the front of the class. It wasn't all plain sailing at school either – she described the teases and taunts of some bullies in her class and the emotional scars they caused. Yet she refused to be pitied or to be considered different. She refused to become downcast, dejected or disappointed. And when the kids would go out to play hopscotch and the like at break time, she was temporarily excluded. But afterwards she would crawl over every square inch of dirt to memorise the moves so that eventually she could join in.

Borghild had such a love of learning. Every evening at home she would hold books up to the corner of her eye to read and she liked nothing better than her parents reading to her. She described her attempts to learn the piano at age nine, despite her obvious difficulty in reading the music. And this persistence and love of learning paid off when she was awarded a scholarship to university at a time when very few women got third level education. This was followed by a Masters degree in English at Columbia University, and the award of a scholarship in Norway. This led to a career in teaching and to Borghild becoming the author of seventeen books. She described her challenges as a teacher, overcoming adversity, giving weekly radio book reviews and becoming an advocate for children's literature.

Nine years later, despite the fact that she had been teaching while practically blind, she was appointed Professor of Journalism at Sioux Falls University in South Dakota. She described how she would memorise the location of each student in her classes and utilised a breathtaking array of memory techniques to compensate for and hide the fact that she couldn't see.

Her journey was a really inspiring story of courage and determination. Except that wasn't the end, it was simply the end of the beginning. Borghild endured what seemed like a severe setback when she lost what little vision she had remaining. Then a new revolutionary operation became available for her at the Mayo Clinic. As a result, she could now see forty times more clearly from her left eye. A whole new exciting world of wonder and beauty opened up to her. And she was so grateful for the simple things in life. She described the beauty in ordinary things like seeing the reflection of the rainbow in the soap suds and looking out the kitchen window at the blackbird beating his wings or observing the phases of the moon. And she described her heartfelt gratitude, not just for her improved sight, but for all the experiences of her life. 'Dear father in heaven, I thank thee, I thank thee.' Here was a person who faced her fears, forged ahead, and found a way through adversity even when, at times, there appeared to be none. Along the way, Borghild Dahl embraced joy and healing as well as heartbreak and discouragement, all with equal measure. Never ever giving up on her dreams, she saw everything through the lens of gratitude.

The Power of Gratitude

Gratitude is a new way of seeing, of sensing and really appreciating all the gifts and goodness in your life. The realisation that right here, right now in the present moment, you have all you need for total fulfilment. The Greek philosopher, Epictetus, wrote that 'he is a wise man who does not grieve for the things which he has not, but rejoices for those which he has.'

Quite simply, gratitude means choosing to appreciate what you have in your life and being thankful, rather than simply taking things for granted. Cultivating the art of gratitude creates meaning and value in everyday situations and relationships, and is a key ingredient in the recipe for a life of contentment.

Gratitude is an awareness of, and appreciation for, all the good things in your life and in the world. Acknowledging and continuing to want what you have leads to appreciation, whereas striving to simply have what you want depreciates the value of what you already have. Celebrating your blessings makes your life feel more abundant which can lead to an upward spiral of well-being.

I think of gratitude as being like emotional dynamite, explosive in terms of how it can transform your happiness and well-being. That's how powerful gratitude is, real emotional TnT. (Thinking about all the things in your life you have to be grateful for and giving thanks!) In fact, both words, think and thank, share the same etymological root – thinking is thanking! Chesterton, the nineteenth-century English writer, maintained that giving thanks was the highest form of thought, and that gratitude is happiness doubled by wonder.

True gratitude goes beyond the simple, pleasant but sometimes superficial please and thank you when you are served a cup of coffee or when someone holds a door open for you. True gratitude is more than good manners and politeness; it is thoughtful, intentional and unscripted – a thank you with meaning. It is the habit of appreciating other people, of expressing thanks for human kindness in all its forms – life's little things that at the end of the day really aren't quite so little. Gratitude is about becoming attuned to the many gifts and blessings that come your way; it's a process, part and parcel of personal growth.

Expressing gratitude is a conscious choice to focus on abundance rather than scarcity; to channel your energy and attention towards what is present and working, rather than what is absent and ineffective. Deciding to choose an attitude of gratitude becomes self-perpetuating; over time you will become aware of more and more good things to be grateful for. You develop the cornerstone of an unstoppable attitude. Much more than a feeling, an attitude of gratitude is a fundamental way of life, a foundation stone for real happiness.

Gratitude is heartfelt – this means it comes from the heart. Gratitude is the heart's way of remembering, an integral connection between giving and receiving. Confucius wrote that you should act with kindness but do not expect gratitude. Receiving gratitude is a gift that must be freely given – it can't be forced. Spending time anxiously awaiting its arrival, I call expectancy syndrome!

The art of true gratitude is to want what you have right now in your life, not to simply have what you want. True gratitude allows you to remember and to appreciate all the wonderful things you have in your life and to be grateful for them. It enables you to recognise that you already have everything you need in your life to experience the happy dwarfs and expand your happiness.

Cicero, the Roman philosopher, described gratitude as the greatest of virtues, the parent of all the others. Gratitude not only *feels* good; it inspires you to *do* good for others. Gratitude is good medicine for the mind, body and soul and expressing gratitude has a range of psychological, emotional, physical and interpersonal benefits.

Expressing gratitude strengthens your psychological fitness, boosts your self-esteem and self-worth. When people are sincerely appreciated, their own sense of self-worth and self-confidence is elevated as well. Expressing gratitude can give you a greater sense of purpose and awareness about what is most important. By refocusing attention away from stress and worry, gratitude can help you reframe stressful life experiences in a more positive light, develop more meaning and enhance life satisfaction. You become more resilient, more likely to work towards your goals and more likely to grow. Gratitude fosters forgiveness, as it is harder to feel upset and disappointed with someone you feel grateful towards.

Gratitude is a terrific happiness booster and can increase your capacity for Joy and the other happy dwarfs like Hope,

Enthusiasm and Inspiration. Cultivating an attitude of gratitude can build your empathy, kindness and compassion, encouraging you to care more and generously reach out to support others. As you experience more heartfelt appreciation, you become more optimistic, less materialistic and self-centred. Expressing gratitude is a powerful reminder of all that's good in your life. There is a freedom to gratitude: setting you free from past regrets and future anxieties, free from envy about what you don't have or who you are not. By opening your heart and your mind, gratitude can teach you to savour the moments, and to optimise the happiness, meaning and potential fulfilment that your life contains.

By helping you not take things for granted, the expression of gratitude helps counteract the effects of hedonic adaptation (the process whereby your happiness level returns to its set point over time). A healthy dose of gratitude is a powerful antidote to the poison dwarfs and needless negativity. In fact, many of the seven poison dwarfs, especially Anger and Envy, are simply incompatible with a deep feeling of gratitude. As a powerful antidote to needless negativity, expressing gratitude can free you from the negative perception of what you don't have or who you are not. It is simply not possible to feel envious, resentful or hostile, and grateful at the same time. Try it and see for yourself!

By expressing gratitude in your journal, you are more likely to exercise more regularly, develop a more healthy lifestyle, and better value your physical health. Expressing gratitude can improve your health in so many ways. You will sleep more soundly, enhance your energy and feel better with your life overall.

Grateful people are more positive, less likely to be anxious or depressed and better liked by others. Existing relationships are strengthened while new ones are more likely to emerge, as you produce feelings of greater connectedness with others.

In terms of your spiritual relationship, connection with your higher power facilitates a sense of awe, an appreciation for what life has to offer, and for what you have to offer the world.

Gratitude Deficiency Syndrome (GDS)

One of the paradoxes about expressing gratitude is that while it makes you happier and healthier, it's not an easy thing to do on a regular basis. Building and maintaining good habits takes work, effort and discipline. We are all creatures of habit and despite our best intentions, we can easily slip back into old ways of doing things. Remember the deep-seated human tendency to take things for granted, to keep doing what you have always done, to simply forget to be grateful. Men, in particular, may believe that to express gratitude implies dependency or weakness and is at odds with the sense of bullet-proof male invincibility.

Negativity bias (the primitive tendency to be more aware of the negative in your life while ignoring or taking for granted what's going well) can be a real barrier to expressing gratitude, as can the myriad of negative thinking patterns. It's useful to appreciate that many of those things in your life that you may now take for granted were once things highly sought after by you. Schopenhauer, the German philosopher, wrote that one of the greatest tragedies in humanity is this tendency to focus on what's lacking rather than what's present – what I call scarcity mentality. Cultivating gratitude can allow you to overcome this scarcity mentality; the deep-rooted fear and belief that there is not enough for everyone, that the 'pie of life' is limited in size with only a fixed number of pieces. So if you are winning, I must be losing – the win/lose mentality. Better instead to consider win/win, abundance, a bigger pie!

Practical ways to grow gratitude in your life

Lack of awareness of the importance of gratitude is another

genuine barrier to being consistently grateful. Learn to become more self-aware. Set your psychological thermostat to focus on all those things you have to be grateful for, creating an upward spiral of positivity. Use your environment at work or at home to create visual reminders of the many good things that are going on in your life. Keep a picture of your loved ones on your office desk. Create some visual reminders of gratitude in your home and living space. Use photos and other visual reminders of the abundance and blessings. Commit to spending more time with positive people who express gratitude.

Just as a rose in your garden needs to be watered and fed, so too does gratitude need to be nurtured and protected. Expressing gratitude regularly in your journal is a game-changing habit that can transform your life: a kind of Chinese bamboo tree seed for lasting creativity, growth and joy. The journal is probably the most effective strategy to consistently improve your level of gratitude. Writing about those things that you are grateful for can enhance and expand your awareness of the many good things in your life that are already making you happy, a powerful way to boost your positive emotions and happy dwarfs. Crystallising your gratitude on paper gives you context and a sense of meaning and makes it real. Writing down your thoughts about gratitude, as opposed to just thinking about them, is the key; the gift of gratitude is only a gift when it's expressed or given!

Research by Professor Robert Emmens, one of the world's leading positive psychology scholars, a gratitude expert, based at the University of California, Davis and author of *Thanks! How Practicing Gratitude Can Make You Happier,* has found that you can boost your long-term happiness significantly (perhaps by up to 25 per cent) by building the habit of writing regularly about gratitude in your journal. Pick a time that is normally available to you, such as first thing in the morning or last thing at night. Personally, I find first thing in the morning to be the most protected part of the day with the least potential for interruption. Remember it can take sixty-six days to build a new habit; remember to remember.

And for parents with young children, asking them to list three things that went well each night as you tuck them into bed is a great way to build a culture of gratitude and positivity.

From my own experience as well as feedback from patients, I believe that expressing gratitude every day can become a bit monotonous and tedious for many people. This is backed up by research that simply writing about gratitude in your journal just once or twice a week can be enough to ensure that this happiness-inducing habit retains all of its sparkle and zeal.

In your journal, write down the goal of expressing more gratitude. Write down three things that you are genuinely grateful for. Think about your loved ones, specific people who care for you or have made sacrifices for you. Rather than a long list of things, go for depth and describe your gratitude in detail. Reflect on how much someone means to you and be grateful for that relationship. Recognise the ways in which someone has been kind to you. Why are you grateful and in what ways has your life been enriched by the relationship?

Express gratitude for your health; appreciate your ability to see, hear, smell, taste and touch. Express gratitude for being alive, for the very miracle of life itself. Think about some goals that you have achieved, and all the wonderful things in your life. Appreciate the natural environment around you. Consider the ritual of grace before meals, of prayer, of giving thanks to God. Remember any ungrateful thoughts you have, and substitute them with a more grateful thought instead. Consider one thing that you might normally take for granted and don't appreciate.

Writing about some challenges and hard times in your life that you have overcome can evoke strong emotions and a powerful sense of gratitude: ask yourself what have you learned and how you have grown as a person?

Remember that gratitude means wanting what you have; learning to see everything in your life as a gift gives your life more meaning. Variety is the spice of life and, by varying the themes that you focus on, you can continue to be invigorated and energised by the power of expressing gratitude in your journal. Gratitude begets gratitude; the more good things you see in your life to be grateful for, the more good things you will see. Expressing gratitude makes life more abundant, leading to an upward spiral of appreciation.

Think of someone who has been very good to you in the past whom you haven't ever properly thanked – maybe an old teacher, school friend or family member. Consider writing them a gratitude letter: not simply a mere thank you note but a considered and considerate expression of the pleasure and meaning that a particular person and relationship has brought to you, highlighting shared memories, experiences, and their significance. Write three hundred words explaining what the person did for you that you appreciate; how their 'gift' has made a difference; where you are and who you have become as a result. There are so many possibilities and opportunities to write to someone in life: people that have inspired you in some way or helped or supported you at an important time in your life.

Instead of posting the gratitude letter you have written, you can boost your happiness further by delivering it in person and reading it out to the recipient. This is known as the gratitude visit, described so well by Martin Seligman and his team at the University of Pennsylvania. This is where you choose someone from your past, still alive, who has made a major positive impact in your life and to whom you have never fully expressed your thanks. Write them a one-page letter, arrange to meet them face to face, and read out your letter to them slowly and deliberately. See how it makes you feel. Wow! This experience can lead to a significant boost in happiness and to a fall in depressive symptoms with an improvement noted after only a week and maintained up to three months later. The gratitude visit can strengthen any relationship and lead to a significant boost in your happiness and well-being.

I first read about Borghild Dahl several years ago and was so moved by her inspirational story of courage, I simply had to get her book. This wasn't easy as she had died many years earlier and the book was written in the year 1944. Eventually I managed to get my hands on a second-hand signed copy! Her story really inspired me but more importantly it got me thinking about those things that I have been blind to in my own life and that I need to be more grateful for. What might you be blind to in your life that you need to see more clearly through the eyes of gratitude? When was the last time you felt truly grateful? There are 86,400 seconds in any one day: how many have you used to express gratitude?

The Second Commitment:

Kindness and Compassion -
Live to Give

When I think of giving while living, I can recall no finer example than the story of Oseola McCarty, who became known as the washerwoman who touched the world. Born in 1908, she was raised in Hattiesburg, Mississippi, by her grandmother and aunt, who worked as a cleaner. They relied completely on each other. At age eleven, when her aunt became ill, Oseola quit school to look after her and work fulltime as a washerwoman. She never returned to school, something she always regretted as she appreciated the value of real education. In fact she never married, never had children and never even learned to drive, preferring to walk everywhere.

But she loved her work, something that was a real vocation for her, a daily labour of love. She saw her work as a real blessing, her purpose in life. She had precise and exacting standards, preferring her time-tested method of scrubbing her laundry by hand to new-fangled gadgets like washing machines or automatic dryers. Her enthusiasm and energy for her work spread her reputation for quality far and wide in her community. This extraordinary work ethic kept her going daily until age eighty-six when her hands, painfully swollen and gnarled with arthritis, forced her retirement.

Working until that age in such a physical fashion would be considered remarkable by many. But shortly after she retired, McCarty did something even more remarkable. She gave away most of her considerable life savings. You see Oseola had begun to save almost as soon as she started working at age eight. As the money had accumulated in her doll's buggy, this young girl took action and started to save regularly in her local bank. All those dimes, quarters and dollar bills that she got as tips, all those small regular, seemingly insignificant contributions, started to add up, reaching a sum at retirement of $250,000.

Oseola wasn't good with numbers. When she enquired about her life savings, the bank manager put ten coins up on the counter to represent them and asked, 'what would you like to do with them?' She pointed to the first coin and said 'that's for my church, and these next three coins are for my nieces and nephew.' 'And the other six coins?' 'Don't worry, I have something really special planned for those.'

Having set aside just enough to live on, McCarty donated $150,000 to the University of Southern Mississippi to fund scholarships for worthy but needy students seeking the education she never had. Even more remarkably, she decided to give most of it away, not as a bequest, but right now while she was still alive, giving while living. When reminded that the university she was donating to was white-only until the 1960s, she displayed her unwavering commitment and spirit of forgiveness. 'They used to not let black people go out there.

A PRESCRIPTION FOR HAPPINESS

But now they do. And I think they should have it.' Like many philanthropists, McCarty inspired many others to be kind and generous. In fact, over 600 men and women in Hattiesburg and beyond made donations that more than tripled her original endowment. Today, the university presents several full-tuition McCarty scholarships every year. Ted Turner, the media billionaire, was so moved by her generosity that he pledged a billion dollars of his own fortune to the United Nations.

When asked why she didn't spend the money she'd saved on herself, she answered with a smile, 'I am spending it on myself. I am proud that I worked hard and that my money will help young people who worked hard to deserve it. I'm proud that I am leaving something positive in this world. My only regret is that I didn't have more to give.'

Oseola received many awards and honours for her spirit of generosity. She was the first ever recipient of an honorary degree from the University of Southern Mississippi. Harvard University awarded her an honorary doctorate in 1996. President Clinton presented her with a Presidential Citizens medal, America's second highest civilian award, and she also won the United Nations Avicenna Medal for educational commitment. She made the cover of Time *magazine; 'The washerwoman who rocked the world' was the headline. Perhaps the key for Oseola was that she really understood that giving is its own pleasure and that she didn't have to save the whole world to make a meaningful difference.*

Her only stated wish was that she might live long enough to attend the graduation of a student who made it through college because of her gift. And this she did. This first beneficiary of her gift, a Hattiesburg girl named Stephanie Bullock, promptly adopted McCarty as a surrogate grandmother!

'I can't do everything. But I can do something to help somebody. And what I can do I will do.' Oseola McCarty's recognition was highly deserved, not only for her own

accomplishments, but as an outstanding example of the potential possibility that lies within you to make a difference in the lives of others. Thank you, Oseola, for having the courage to live your own life on your own terms in such an inspirational manner.

Give to Live

How do you view kindness: as a weakness or strength of character? The hectic pace of modern life means that many people get caught up in the hustle and bustle, so busy being busy with little or no time left to stop and be kind to others.

Kindness and the act of giving to others brings on the happy dwarfs, especially Love, and Hope, so good for your physical health. This may be as a result of kindness activating the vagus nerve, the longest nerve in the body, which controls the body's relaxation response. The vagus nerve also interacts with nerves that regulate emotional expression, eye contact and reception to human speech, influencing release of cardio-protective hormones like oxytocin. This encourages closeness and bonding and releases nitric oxide which dilates blood vessels and lowers blood pressure.

Giving and receiving are both part of the same universal flow of energy, the yin and the yang of life. Emerson, the American philosopher, wrote about one of the most beautiful compensations of this life being that no man can sincerely try to help another without helping himself. Expressing kindness to others can strengthen your psychological fitness, physical health and relationships as well as being a terrific happiness booster. When you commit to become kinder and more compassionate, you develop more perspective and become better able to see your own problems in a more realistic light. Kindness encourages you to be more open and future-orientated, feeling better and more confident about your own intrinsic good nature. You see yourself as being more caring, compassionate and altruistic; reducing feelings of hostility and helplessness. From a very practical viewpoint, kindness helps to relieve distress about the misfortunes of others. Kindness helps you to see the world as a more generous and caring place, building trust and becoming a catalyst for positive change. Kindness allows you to feel more grateful and appreciative for what you already have; it boosts your self-esteem and brings out the best in you. When I reflect on the power of kindness and compassion, I think of those wise words of the Eastern poet Rumi:

'When you are dead, seek for your resting place not in the earth, but in the hearts of men.'

Kindness satisfies a core human need for strong connection. It creates more positive social interactions and the opportunity to make new friends. Of course, this can become self-perpetuating, as expressing kindness makes it more likely that people will appreciate you, be grateful for your kindness and support you in return.

Plato, the philosopher, wrote, 'Be kind, for everyone you meet is fighting a hard battle.'

Being kinder and more connected to others opens your heart, building your empathy and compassion. So, if you want more love in your life, give more love to others and be more loving. If you want more joy, be more joyful. If you want more attention, give more attention to others.

Giving is a double-edged sword of positivity, evoking feelings of gratitude in the giver as well as in the receiver. Happier people tend to be kinder, more compassionate and willing to help others while a commitment to become kinder and more compassionate is a great way to feel happier. Kindness boosts happiness and can boost feelings of joyfulness, realistic optimism and resilience. Kindness creates an upward spiral of happiness and well-being. Being kind can bring on a 'helper's high': an initial feeling of euphoria followed by a longer period of emotional well-being and contentment. Kindness also gives people a strong sense that they are doing something that matters which feeds into their values, mission and sense of meaning. So get into the happiness-inducing habit of giving something to everyone you meet – even if it is only the gift of your attention or your smile.

The ripple effect of kindness

Mark Twain once wrote that kindness is 'a language that the deaf can hear and the blind can see.' It's that powerful! Kindness can be highly contagious and can spread just like a virus. Experiencing kindness can give you a feel-good factor, encouraging you to go out and do something to help others. Think of the expanding ripple that spreads outwards across a pond when a pebble is thrown in. Kindness can start a similar chain reaction of positivity: your committing to be more kind to others can lead others to be more kind and generous. So forget survival of the fittest, it's kindness that counts! You are hardwired to be kind. In fact this profoundly compassionate nature and deep inbuilt capacity for caring may confer significant survival advantages as a species.

More recently, Nicholas Christakis and James Fowler, authors of the book *Connected*, found that when one person gives money to others in a game where people have the opportunity to cooperate, in future games the recipients become more likely to give their own money away. This 'learned kindness' habit has been shown to persist in that you don't go back to your former selfish or less kind self.

In fact, just like positive emotion, kindness can spread out to three degrees of separation, impacting not only on your friends, but on your friends' friends and on your friends' friends' friends! As a result, your giving may inspire people you don't even know to give, causing a cascading effect of kindness. Within your 'bubble of three degrees of separation' are thought to be about a thousand people. So your leadership in choosing to be more kind can impact on a thousand people in a positive way. How exciting is that?

Pay it forward is a concept whereby your kindness to someone else is returned, not to you, but by that person being kind to someone else, passing it forward like a baton in a relay race.

I was told a great version of this recently at a seminar I gave in Ireland on happiness. While we were talking about random acts of kindness a lady in the audience voluntarily shared her story. She had been stuck at a cash machine a few mornings earlier when, much to her dismay, her bank card wouldn't work. She became angry and frustrated, knowing there was money in her account, which she desperately needed to put petrol into her car to get to work on time. She was frantic with worry that her job might be on the line if she was late. What was she going to do? Just then, a lady behind her in the queue tapped her on the shoulder and gave her €20! 'Go get yourself to work!' When she asked how and when she could repay her, the lady said: 'Don't worry about me; help someone else instead.' Ask yourself when was the last time you helped someone without expecting anything in return?

Practical Keys to Kindness

An act of kindness is anything that will benefit another person or make them happy which involves some input of time or effort by you. You may well be thinking as you are reading this: sure I'm kind all the time, a regular Santa Claus, why would I need to practice random acts of kindness? Research by Sonya Lyubomirsky, a brilliant positive psychologist based in California, has found that five random acts of kindness done once a week over a six-week period can significantly improve your happiness. Doing the five acts of kindness on one single day makes you more self-attuned to your thoughts, feelings and actions that day, more aware of being in the moment in terms of your time and more appreciative of the impact that your words or actions are having, not only on other people but on yourself.

Doing the five acts of kindness over the entire week instead doesn't seem to work as well, as their positive impact tends to be overshadowed and diluted by everything else that is going on in your life. So committing to express kindness towards others really can boost your happiness; giving really does start the receiving process! I don't know about you, but I find that the days, weeks, even months just seem to fly by. Make an appointment with yourself in your journal to complete five random acts of kindness – once a week!

There are simply so many ways to express kindness. Use your journal to come up with a list of different ways in which you can express random acts of kindness. Keep them fresh and invigorating and remember variety is the spice of life. Consider things that mightn't be part of your daily routine but which can make a difference, such as letting someone go ahead of you in line, doing chores that you normally don't do, or helping a stranger in need. Examples of five random acts of kindness would include buying a stranger a coffee; commit to making a phone call or writing a letter to someone you know who is lonely; renewing contact with an old friend; donating what you can regularly to a reputable charity of your choice; volunteer your time, talents or energy to support others. Consider doing something with a friend or two with similar interests; this can help with motivation and accountability.

Try them and see for yourself how this regular kindness day can become a new tipping point for your happiness and well-being. So what are you waiting for? Remember, by being more kind, you have the potential to boost your own happiness as well as to spread some happiness to others. You truly can help to make the world a better place.

When was the last time you gave or received a hug? A wise person once wrote that 'Hugs help to make the healthy healthier, the happy happier, and the most secure among us even more so. Hugs are not only nice, they are needed. A hug can make happy days happier and impossible days possible.'

Hugs may just be one of those secret ingredients to a healthier life, helping to soothe away stress, foster feelings of closeness and warmth, and they are an excellent friendship booster. Think about someone who might feel better from a hug today. Start by giving your partner, children or someone special a hug at least once a day. Everyone can benefit from hugs, no matter what age. Never make assumptions that someone would appreciate a hug; respect someone's personal space and always ask for permission first! Hugs have been shown to boost positive emotion, improve mood, and at the same time let go of some of those poison dwarfs, especially Fear and Anxiety. Hugging can help your body produce more oxytocin; a feel-good hormone in your blood which causes a bonding or caring response in people, helping you feel more relaxed and at ease. So consider a hug a day, to fortify you against the stress of the day ahead and fill you with emotional vitality.

Engaging with your community through volunteering can be a real game changer for your happiness and well-being. What's more, the overall health benefits of volunteering can be enormous. Volunteering can take many forms, including charity or community work, serving your local school, or giving a gift of your time or resources, even anonymously. Volunteering can be the glue that binds a community together, building connections between people and, in turn, helping to make the world a better place. It makes sense that feeling good would be a natural consequence of volunteering and reaching out to help others.

Volunteering can improve your self-esteem and self-confidence and make you more resilient and likely to persist with your goals. It can give you a natural sense of accomplishment, enhance life satisfaction and encourage a more positive view on life. Volunteering can improve mood, lower anxiety and reduce the risk of depressive symptoms, keeping you outward-looking rather than becoming introspective and self-obsessed. It can allow you to develop new skills or interests, avail of new experiences, become a more rounded and balanced person and help to fulfil several important psychological needs, including the need to feel valued.

Volunteering affords the opportunity to develop new friendships, expand your contacts, and create new social networks as you get to learn more about people and life itself. Giving to your community through volunteering strengthens your sense of interdependence and of connectedness and these are strong factors in increasing happiness. Building relationships at many levels helps you feel more engaged and connected, protecting you from stress and depressive symptoms when you face new challenges. By committing to a shared activity, you get to meet people with common interests. Volunteering can also strengthen relationships within organisations, creating a shared common purpose, building positivity and enhancing job satisfaction.

As you develop helping habits, volunteering can improve your health. Volunteering your time, talents and energy can be a terrific happiness booster, bringing laughter and smiles in its wake! Helper's high is a well-described emotional boost of emotional contentment experienced by volunteers, who feel energised and even euphoric with enriched meaning in their lives after helping others. Volunteering can be an engaging escape from the day-to-day routine: a natural antidote to negativity: and those poison dwarfs. The happiness spillover effect in your personal and professional life from volunteering boosts positivity by bringing on the happy dwarfs. Hoping for the possibility of a better future might be just the emotional tonic your life needs to get to the next level of well-being. Making your community, your nation and your world a better place is a 365-day-a-year responsibility – so make a difference and consider volunteering. There are so many worthy organisations out there waiting for you to lend them a hand, so go on, what are you waiting for? Make that call today and see how good it can make you feel.

The Third Commitment:

Great Relationships – A Recipe for Real Contentment

In Irish mythology and folklore, there was a faraway land called Tír na nÓg, or Land of the Young. This was a magical place of abundance, health and everlasting youth, where no one grew old and where dreams were fulfilled. When Oisín, one of the fabled Fianna warriors and Niamh (from the Otherworld) fall in love, she brings him to Tír na nÓg, on a magical horse that can run over water. Having spent what seems like three years there, Oisín returns home to find that three hundred years have passed!

Even in Ireland, we know such a place of everlasting youth to be nothing more than the romantic dreams of a Celtic legend! But just for a moment, imagine a real place where living to age ninety and beyond is an expectation rather than an exception.

A PRESCRIPTION FOR HAPPINESS

A real place where the timetables and deadlines of modern life melt away in a timeless vacuum of unity with nature and the seasons. And more importantly, where there is a deep sense of connection and celebration with other people. Not a 'me' place but a 'we' place! A fairy tale, another Celtic legend, you might say! But such a place does really exist, where happiness and well-being is the norm.

Welcome to the tiny Greek island of Icaria, known by repute for its health-enhancing vitality for more than 2,500 years. Its location in the North Aegean Sea off the Turkish coastline and an absence of natural harbours kept it outside of main shipping lanes and, as a result, forced its people to be self-sufficient for centuries. Some interesting statistics: nearly one in every three of these island inhabitants become nonogenerians (living to age ninety and beyond). And I don't simply mean surviving longer but really thriving – socialising, enjoying sex, sipping wine well into their sunset years. Dementia is rare and depression is far less common than in the Western world, as are age-adjusted rates of heart disease or cancer. And why is this the case? Their secret appears to be a life of rich simplicity and a supportive network of strong relationships. A place where eating is a social event, where daily naps are the norm and the simple antioxidant-rich Mediterranean diet is full of locally sourced green vegetables, beans, lentils and bread, olive oil, herbal teas, coffee, wine, goats' milk and honey (a local panacea for well-being). A place where the hilly terrain encourages exercise and where green exercise, in the form of gardening, is highly valued. A place where there is a different relationship with time (no one wears watches). Perhaps above all, a place where close interpersonal relationships are the norm with young and not-so-young cherished equally.

Icaria is known as one of the 'Blue Zones', areas of the world that have unusually high clusters of elderly people. Other Blue

Zone areas, described in detail in National Geographic Fellow, Dan Buettner's book, *The Blue Zones*, include mountain villages in the Nuoro province in Sardinia, the islands of Okinawa in Japan, and Loma Linda, California. Research from these areas has found that these elderly people share several common features in their lifestyle. These include putting your family first, staying socially connected and engaged in your community (as well as not smoking, staying physically active and eating a diet rich in greens and legumes). One of the common themes is that people feel included and very much part of their communities, on the inside looking out, rather than on the outside looking in. So, robust relationships with friends, family and community may not only improve the quality of your life by making you happier with fewer health problems, they may also help to prolong your life. Strong relationships provide a protective buffer against stress and negativity and enhance your sense of self-confidence and well-being. They keep you better equipped to prevent general wear and tear of your body and mind. Building strong relationships helps you to be more resilient, recover quicker from illness and sleep better.

Like bread and water, to be accepted and understood among friends is among the most basic of all human needs. Perhaps this need is hardwired into your brain as a key survival mechanism. Primitive man was a hunter-gatherer who lived in groups, shared food and fought off common enemies. His survival skills were not based on speed, aggression or physical prowess; instead, the ability to communicate, collaborate and build strong interpersonal relationships set him apart. There are so many different types of relationships: your partner and loved ones, family, friends, colleagues; relationships in the wider community and, of course, your spiritual relationship. Basically, your life revolves around your relationships as the leading indicator of your well-being. From the Greek philosopher, Aristotle, to the eminent zoologist, Darwin, a compelling case has been made about the real human need to develop strong relationships. The field of positive psychology has shown that really robust relationships are like powerful magnets to attract positivity, forming the basis for a rich, meaningful and flourishing life.

More than two thousand years ago, Aristotle wrote that, without friendship, no happiness is possible. Relationships are a rich source of support for a life of vitality and meaning. Having real friends to provide fun, security and, when needed, the proverbial shoulder to lean against is really important. Friends can provide the support and psychological nourishment required to meet many of your needs, including love and acceptance, certainty, confidence and comfort. They help develop the interpersonal skills and provide the experiences and the 'glue' to support your emotional well-being and happiness.

Human beings are interdependent: neither totally dependent on, nor completely independent from others. And, in this increasingly interdependent world, relationships and networks define who you are. Great relationships are all about the synergy that exists between people, the degree of connectedness and interdependence.

Research by Martin Seligman found that the main difference between happy and very happy people was the presence or absence of strong social relationships. By cultivating the relationships in your life, they can provide you with a well of long-term satisfaction, meaning and significance. They can offer a real psychological boost to support people in reaching more of their potential. There is something unique and special about relationships, something motivating, emotionally elevating and life-enhancing.

A PRESCRIPTION FOR HAPPINESS

The Lessons of Loneliness

In today's digital information age messaging speed is instant, networking opportunities have multiplied and social media is viral. But while the modern era places great importance on communication, actual time with friends is often replaced by Facebook time. Face-to-face communication is so often, now, the exception rather than the expectation.

The letter 'i' in illness represents isolation, and the crucial letters in wellness are the first two letters 'we'. Us, together. Absence makes the heart grow fonder, as the saying goes, but it can also make the heart weaker! Quality relationships are integral to your well-being; if you don't have them then the health of your heart can suffer and you can fall apart physically, psychologically and emotionally. A wise man once said to be grateful for your friends for they are the gardeners that make your soul blossom. Simply being around other people is not enough; rather the quality of the relationship will determine whether or not a person feels lonely. People with meaningful friendships derive higher levels of well-being and are healthier and more engaged in their lives. By contrast, the absence of any close friendships increases the likelihood of depression, boredom and loneliness.

Understanding loneliness can help you appreciate the fundamental importance of relationships in determining your happiness in life. There is a big difference between being alone and being lonely; you may choose to spend time alone, but you don't choose to be lonely. Some of the happiest and most fulfilled people on the planet spend considerable time alone and won't consider themselves to be lonely for one second. Being alone can be a wonderful opportunity to reflect, relax and recharge.

Loneliness, on the other hand, can cause you to feel empty, alone and unwanted. It is really a negative state of mind: an emotional response to the perception of being alone, excluded, apart from the crowd. As a universal human emotion, experiencing temporary loneliness from time to time is part and parcel of being human: who doesn't remember that relationship breakup, the party you weren't invited to, the first days in a new job? One of the best ways to understand the health benefits of relationships is to see what happens when loneliness sets in; when your relationships are deficient, lacking or absent in some way. Persistent loneliness can have a wide range of adverse effects on your happiness, psychological and physical health. This impact of loneliness on well-being has been described in detail in the book *Loneliness: Human Nature and the Need for Social Connection* by the psychologist John T. Cacioppo.

Loneliness is a hidden killer and can increase the risk of premature death. Higher levels of circulating stress hormones in your system over many years put strain on your heart and blood vessels, increasing the risk of heart disease, blood clots and stroke. Being lonely can quite literally cause a broken heart! Higher levels of cumulative wear and tear increase the risk of premature ageing and functional decline, increasing the risk of falls. Being persistently lonely may have health risks comparable to the health risks from smoking cigarettes, obesity and high blood pressure!

Loneliness can trigger feelings of fatigue, increase your sensitivity to pain and can make you less likely to adopt a healthy lifestyle in terms of diet, exercise habits and alcohol consumption. Being lonely can also affect your decision-making, your memory and overall brain health, increasing the risk of dementia. Your sleep quality can be affected in that you feel less refreshed after sleep both physically and psychologically.

Loneliness brings on the poison dwarfs, especially Anxiety and Sadness, which dance around in your brain creating an emotional soundtrack of negativity; this background noise is not only unsettling but which can eat away at your emotional happiness and well-being. The result: a downward spiral of doom and gloom and a state of mind that makes it more challenging to reach out and build relationships even though that is what's most needed.

Being lonely can affect your self-esteem, lower your self-confidence and undermine learning and memory. One of the great benefits of relationships is their ability to buffer and protect you against the damaging effects of stress. Loneliness increases the levels of negative stress and distress. On the other hand loneliness can also be a major trigger of mental health conditions such as depression and alcohol dependency. Low self-esteem and lack of self-confidence can result in social withdrawal, which can exacerbate loneliness and increase the risk of suicide.

If you feel lonely, be aware of these feelings as a sign you may need to strengthen your relationships. Be really clear about what persistent loneliness can mean for your health, happiness and well-being.

Strengthening ties that matter

There are areas of the brain called mirror neurons that encourage you to copy or imitate your friends and those people you spend time with. Initially discovered through research on macaque monkeys, mirror neurons may be responsible not only for your tendency to mimic the feelings and actions of those people you meet but also for the development of human culture. Be mindful of the people you spend time with; you become your associations. You are always being blended by your experiences; in this mirroring effect, you can take on the habits, beliefs and even the mannerisms of the people you surround yourself with. It's as if your brain will practise doing something that you have just seen which makes it easier for you to carry out that behaviour in the future. The most important determinants of who you will be in five years' time are the self-development work you do and the people you associate and spend most time with.

In their book *Connected: The Amazing Power of Social Networks and How They Shape Our Lives*, authors Christakis and Fowler describe how you are much more likely to have a healthy lifestyle if your friends have a healthy lifestyle. Monkey see, monkey do! If your best friend takes lots of aerobic exercise, you are more likely to be physically active. Conversely if a close friend of yours smokes or is obese, you are much more likely to smoke or become obese. Birds of a feather flock together!

Did you know that a simple analysis of a fifteen-minute conversation between you and your partner may accurately predict the health of that relationship? That's what John Gottman has found through his pioneering research into the success or failure of marriage and described in his book *The Seven Principles for Making Marriage Work*. By analysing videos of hundreds of couples in conversation, he was able to predict, with ninety-four per cent accuracy, the chances of staying happily married or developing problems. His key finding was that numbers matter. Five positive feelings, emotions or comments such as feeling valued, affirmed, and appreciated are needed to counterbalance each episode of negativity (the 5:1 ratio of happy to poison dwarfs). Happy couples build positive spirals that focus on positivity, both in their verbal and non-verbal communication. They tend to express their needs positively in terms of what they want rather than what they don't want. It is important to state your feelings, clearly and objectively, without blame, without judging.

This 5:1 ratio between positive and negative interactions is the basis for flourishing relationships. If there isn't enough positivity to counteract the negative then there can be a change in how you perceive things. You may start to see things differently (in a more negative light) which can change how you think, feel and behave. This can lead to more defensive, negative behaviour and a downward spiral.

According to the late Mother Teresa, there is more hunger for love and appreciation in this world than for bread. Small things are the big things; relationships are cultivated and developed by small acts of kindness, positivity and love. It's the little things that often matter the most. Small acts of kindness done with great love. Happily married couples got on well when they were not fighting (every couple fights from time to time) but it is the small, seemingly insignificant exchanges, pleasantries and mutual interests that build a relationship. Gottman found that the quality of a friendship, the sense of shared purpose and meaning, counts for the majority of overall marital satisfaction. Couples in healthy flourishing relationships need shared experiences to grow and spend more time together (on average an extra five hours per week). Actions speak louder than words so demonstrate that your relationship is important to you by making it a priority to spend more time with your partner.

'Benefit of the doubt' can be seen as a sort of oil to grease the wheels of your relationships; all relationships that flourish need patience, understanding, tolerance and, at times, forgiveness. You need to be able to give and receive the benefit of the doubt; after all, nobody's perfect, right! One of the key changes in dysfunctional relationships is this loss of tolerance, when one partner stops giving the other the benefit of the doubt, leading to a self-perpetuating downward negative spiral. There is a collapse in positive emotion and the very foundations of the relationship begin to crack. The poison dwarfs are highly contagious and can do real damage to the long-term health of relationships. So as one member becomes highly stressed, this stress transfers quickly to the other, leading to an emotional hijacking – a tsunami of negativity. Negative people keep you small or stuck in your comfort zone, draining your energy, chipping away at your confidence.

Gottman has described personal criticism, contempt, disgust and stonewalling as 'The Four Horsemen of the Apocalypse' resulting in relationship breakdown.

Personal criticism, in sporting terms, is playing the man not the ball! Being critical of a certain behaviour is an assertion of your emotional intelligence; you might complain about a particular action or behaviour a person did or did not do. For example, 'When you forget to put out the bins, it makes me feel you don't care about me.' In this case, you are criticising your partner's inaction and how it made you feel. Personal criticism is different; it is up close and personal, making the recipient of the criticism feel negative. Example: 'You are just so self-centred and selfish. You can't do anything I ask you. It just proves I can't trust you.' Personal criticism brings on the poison dwarfs like Guilt, Anger and Anxiety and their cousins; you know where those guys bring you to and it isn't the Promised Land! Contempt is a mixture of anger, disgust and scorn and can be the most destructive feature of all in a relationship. It is communicated not just by what's said and the tone of voice but also by powerful non-verbal communication messages such as sneering, rolling of the eyes, turning the head away and other such negative facial expressions. Disgust is where even the smallest comment can trigger a severe overreaction and a potentially catastrophic shift in the nature of a relationship. When feelings are hurt constantly, the proverbial molehills are turned into mountains and small issues become major battles. Negative behaviour patterns such as arguing, hostility, sarcasm, and rejection expressed towards a partner can cause negative feelings to spiral out of control, leading to emotional hijackings. Stonewalling is emotional withdrawal from a relationship, preventing forgiveness, reconciliation or an opportunity for renewal and a fresh start.

Building relationships is essential to maintain your psychological fitness and expand your happiness. Have a plan to build your relationships. Consider the following pointers as potential ingredients for your recipe to produce flourishing relationships in all aspects of your life. Each of the relationships in your life is unique, both in terms of the strengths your friend brings to the relationship and what you bring. Use your journal as an opportunity to reflect on and review these relationships. Keep a record in your journal of the people you spend time with. Are your current friends people that inspire and encourage you or do they talk negatively and bring you down? Remember the powerful contagious effect of negative emotion and the destructive potential of toxic relationships. Realise that you are too important and special to allow yourself to be dragged down by others.

The Golden Rule in history down through the ages and recognised in the wisdom literature, across many cultures and traditions from Confucius to Christianity, can be described as follows: 'Do to others what you would have them do unto you.' Or 'Don't do to others what you wouldn't want them to do to you.' This is a timeless truth: to be willing to see things from the other person's point of view, to give the benefit of the doubt, to treat others as you would like to be treated! Always seek first to understand, then to be understood. This yin and yang of life is a two-way process. Actions speak louder than words; follow through on your commitments and keep your promises.

Making time for your important relationships and friends allows your relationships to deepen and become richer. Create experiences that are mutually enjoyable: maybe exercising together, watching a match, sharing a meal. Be generous with your time; become a better listener and make the time to really listen to your friends. The quality of all of your relationships can be enhanced if you consistently act in line with your values which, in turn, can make your life more meaningful, enjoyable and fulfilling.

Consider volunteering, community service or another activity that you enjoy; these are great opportunities to cultivate shared interests and to develop new friendships and social interactions. The quality of your friendships can be a powerful investment in your well-being and life satisfaction. Investing time in your relationships is one of the best investments you can make; by investing time regularly with the right people, you are less likely to spend time with the wrong people. Just like compound interest, this is an investment that can grow with long-term sustainable benefits for your happiness, well-being and life satisfaction.

Be more communicative; express your feelings, become a crystal-clear communicator. Be more empathic and a better listener. Being a good listener is really all about paying attention, so that the person communicating with you feels not only listened to but heard, valued and respected. Listen with your ears and your heart; don't be a mind reader or expect others to read your mind. Remember great communicators are made, not born; it's something you have to work at.

Use your skills of active listening and empathy to communicate clearly, concisely and honestly. So ask more open-ended questions and use more eye contact. Better communication cultivates openness and trust. Better communication supports the constructive control of conflict, values the finding of solutions to life's challenges and contributes to the strength of a relationship. Having the psychological air to express your thoughts, feelings and opinions is important to allow any meaningful relationship to grow and develop.

Be encouraging and supportive of the goals and dreams of

your partner and friends; make their happiness and well-being a priority. Be creative and think outside the box; developing a new shared hobby or interest like a new language, gardening, or travel can strengthen relationships.

Be more forgiving and less judgemental; holding grudges just drains your energy. Be dependable and true to your word. Trust is a magic ingredient for the chemistry of relationships. Give your friends the psychological space to grow.

Take action and invest time and energy into your relationships. Be patient and persevere: Rome wasn't built in a day! Be willing to make a few positive changes and have a more positive attitude in all aspects of your relationships. The choice is yours; enjoy the happiness that comes with it. Be realistic in your expectations; relationships are an integral part of happiness and well-being, but they are not everything so don't expect them to be the panacea for life's challenges.

Be yourself; it's much easier and so much more fun in the long run. Build your resilience and focus on positive thoughts which bring on the happy dwarfs that lead to positive results in your life. Remember you are responsible for how you feel. Build your self-esteem by taking ownership of your own happiness and well-being. The late Jim Rohn, motivational speaker and author, put it so well when he wrote that 'I'll take care of me for you if you'll take care of you for me.'

The foundation stone to realising the potential in your friendships and relationships is to be grateful for and appreciate the positive roles that people already do play in your life. Focus on the strengths of your friends rather than their faults; support and stand up for them, honour them in their absence. Focus on what you bring to a friendship or relationship; giving starts the receiving process. If you want more friends in your life, be more friendly! Don't just sit back and expect friends to come into your life; get out there and make it happen. Just like beautiful plants in your garden, friendships need to be cultivated and developed and this requires special care and planning. Work on building your friendships and relationships and spend more time with the people who build you up. Surround yourself with people who will encourage and support you; people who will challenge you to raise your game and keep on improving, to become all that you can be.

The Fourth Commitment:

Goals That Allow You to Grow

Sometime in November 2006 I decided to move forward with my written goal of running a marathon. Even though I'd written this goal down, I still didn't believe I was capable of achieving it. You see I believed back then that marathon running was for 'other' types of people, people who were not only fitter and stronger than me but also people who had more self-belief not to mention the time commitments. 'Excusitis' was rampant in my head until I spoke to one of my friends who had done the Dublin marathon before and was itching to go again. Before I knew it we had both signed up with The Children's Hospital in Dublin to run the New York Marathon the following November with a team led by the legendary Eamonn Coghlan – the first man aged over forty to run a mile in under four minutes. Exalted company indeed! So we downloaded a detailed training plan from the New

A PRESCRIPTION FOR HAPPINESS

York marathon website and we were all set to start in the New Year. I remember those cold January winter nights, jogging three, four, five miles at a time, building slowly, steadily. After a few weeks I noticed I was getting fitter and stronger and also starting to believe in myself more. After all, I had two legs and two arms and could follow a training plan as well as the next guy. Maybe this was possible after all. Ten months later with more than 900 miles 'banked' in the legs including several long twenty-mile runs, we were all set. We boarded the plane for the seven hour flight from Dublin to New York but those poison dwarfs called Fear and his cousin, Anxiety, came with me. They kept me awake the entire night before the race. Adding to all of this was the tragic news that earlier that day an American Olympic hopeful, Ryan Shay, had died suddenly in Central Park during a marathon Olympic trial race (RIP).

On the day of the race, we were all up at 5.30 in the morning to get a bus out to Fort Wadsworth on Staten Island. For more than three hours, all 39,000 of us hung around at the starting line near the approach to the double-decker Verrazano-Narrows bridge. Then we assembled into groups based on our predicted finish time, the real athletes led by Olympic star, Paula Radcliffe, on the lower tier of the bridge, the mere hopefuls like me up on top. At the start line it felt as if I had already run a marathon but hey we were all in the same boat. And the excitement and sheer exhilaration of the occasion took over – the blue sky, the majestic Manhattan skyline in the distance. I remember the start – fighter jets, the Star-Spangled Banner.

The first fifteen miles or so were easy, maybe too easy. Descending the bridge and breezing through the various neighbourhoods of Brooklyn, bands playing, so many people out cheering us on. At the halfway mark (13.1 miles) we crossed the Pulaski Bridge to enter Long Island City, Queens.

A PRESCRIPTION FOR HAPPINESS

After another two and a half miles or so, we crossed the East River via the slow arduous climb up the Queensboro Bridge into Manhattan. Meanwhile Paula Radcliffe had already finished in two hours and twenty-three minutes! And then wham! There it was, sudden, shocking and surreal. The dreaded wall. I had hit it early; they say to expect it at twenty miles but this was only mile sixteen. This shouldn't be happening but it was and every fibre in my body wanted to stop. I had never experienced anything like it; so much psychological pain, physical torture, sheer torment. I remember looking over at the pavement and thinking, I can stop now, I can get away with this, no one will know at home. But deep inside me, I knew I'd know! So I crawled along, through the Bronx, a blurry haze of pain, step after step for what seemed forever but was probably only about forty minutes or so. I kept on going, kept on inching forward. And then I got my second wind and started jogging again. Over the Madison Avenue Bridge and back into Manhattan. Many start but few finish. Forty minutes of pain, a mere drop in the ocean. I refused to lose. Once I got through that wall I knew nothing was going to stop me. I wasn't going to quit. Down through Harlem. Many start but few finish. Keep on going, into Central Park at the southern end, swarming with a sea of spectators. Columbus Circle. And on the horizon, the finish line, like the proverbial oasis in the desert. Crossing the line. A brief moment in time but timeless for me. Words can't properly describe the flood of emotions, the rush, the feelings of exhaustion intertwined with exhilaration. I recall being given a goodie bag containing water, and a small chocolate bar. I never realised chocolate could taste so good. I was overcome with sensual experience as I devoured it greedily.

And then the medal. When they put the medal around my neck it meant so much to me. Not as a fashion accessory to parade around Time Square that night but for what this medal represented. You see I'd set what was, for me, a big goal. I'd worked hard towards it, had moments along the way when I doubted myself and on the day itself, almost quit when so close to finishing. But I had kept going, refused to lose, and with a fair wind at my back and that little element of Irish luck I'd got there in the end. And it felt so good, every inch of that journey. What this marathon represented to me in the weeks and months ahead was the power of possibility, really appreciating that we all have so much untapped potential within us. And it got me asking myself all sorts of interesting questions, like what other goals can I work towards in my life with self-belief and the courage to start?

And what might you achieve in your life if you believe in yourself and have the courage to face your fears and simply start?

Reaching Beyond Yourself

Do you want to be healthier and happier? Do you want more passion and purpose? Do you want stronger relationships, and more success in your life? If the answer to these questions is yes, then set some goals consistent with the person you are on the inside (your values)! Both personally and professionally, I have learned that identifying and working towards goals that are both pleasurable and meaningful is a key way to expand your happiness.

By 'goal setting', I am not talking about daydreams, castles in the air, or vague plans for your future. Unwritten goals are just fantasies; the fairy godmother will sort those out! Real goals are dreams that are being acted upon and set by people who are not just pleasantly interested in something but passionately committed to it. This purposeful planning, writing down and taking steps towards your goals on a regular basis, is a serious business that can pay real dividends in terms of your happiness and well-being.

In short, setting goals can be a prescription for achievement in life, a road map that can take you to places that few people even dream of. So set goals that light the fire within you, that brighten the path in front of you, that radiate courage, confidence and conviction in your direction. Set goals that galvanise your energy, fill you with excitement, and with the power of passionate possibility. Set goals big enough to command your thoughts, inspire your hopes and that in the process of working towards them, support your becoming somebody worth becoming.

Being able to set and work towards goals consistent with your values supports your growing into the person you are capable of becoming, a key ingredient in the recipe for lifelong happiness and success.

We all have choices to make. I have learned from my own experiences about the new possibilities that arise from clarifying your goals, writing them down, stating them positively and working towards them. The most important thing is the person you become while you are working towards something that's important to you. And of course once you are fortunate enough to achieve and realise some of your goals, then you need more goals to work towards!

Goal setting can give you a feeling of control and ownership over the direction of your life, something to work towards and look forward to, the belief that what you are doing really matters. When you set a meaningful goal, you are beginning with the end in mind. You have decided what you want to achieve and how you are going to get there. This process of having a future purpose can give you so much enhanced enjoyment of the present moment.

The modern world is full of distraction, draining your energy and distracting your focus from those decisions that are important for you. Goal setting allows you to exert distraction control in your life – to switch off the negative noise, to psychologically shield yourself from the distracters and distractions. It allows you to apply laser-like focus to the vital few as opposed to the trivial many; it encourages and enables action, achievement and results as opposed to simply being busy. Because you are now focused on what is important, decision-making becomes easier. Quite simply, setting goals allows you to get more done, to be more effective in what you do and to become a peak performer.

There's no point in climbing the ladder of life only to find that it's leaning against the wrong wall! Heightened awareness of what is important for you can give you the clarity that leads to better results in your life. Goal setting can free you up to enjoy the here and now, to focus your full attention on making the most of where you are right now.

The discipline that comes from setting and working towards these value-laden goals can set you free, to become the best possible version of yourself. I believe that it is so important to align your goals to your values, so that what you are working towards gives you real meaning and a sense of fulfilment.

Goal setting is an opportunity to show leadership and inspire others, to become a leader in your own life rather than simply following the crowd. Actions *do* speak louder than words.

Of course, goal setting can give you better structure and meaning in your life through deadlines, timetables and responsibilities as well as the opportunity to develop new skills, and put you on the path to continuous improvement, the journey towards mastery. Goal setting can strengthen your character, by promoting a longer term perspective on your life. In life, everyone has challenges and crises, ups and downs, from time to time. If you remain committed to your goals during these crises, it can help you deal with them much more positively.

Setting goals can support the golden egg of great physical health. As you work towards and accomplish challenging goals that stretch you, you boost your self-esteem and self-confidence and strengthen your psychological fitness. Goal setting can strengthen your relationships. The friends and support networks that you can develop as part of the process of setting goals and engaging with others can be really terrific for your well-being. You can derive so much more enjoyment and exhilaration from and enthusiasm for life. As you become more connected to others, you help your life to flourish. Setting goals can cultivate the happy dwarfs, inject positive emotion and bring a sense of fun and fulfilment to virtually everything you do.

Setting goals for your psychological fitness, emotional vitality, physical health and relationships is a great way of investing in you. Self-investment is the biggest and most rewarding type of investment that you can make. While self-investment may not build your net wealth, it will definitely build your net worth. You expect 100 per cent quality in the products you buy and the services you use every day of your life so why not expect 100 per cent from yourself? Planning ahead like this allows you to set goals that complement rather than compete with each other. For example, the goal of becoming physically fitter by taking more exercise can also build psychological fitness, strengthen relationships and expand your happiness – a real win-win.

Life without Goals

The paradox of setting goals is that it sounds so simple and yet so few people do it! Of course I am not saying that you cannot be successful without written goals. Many people are! You might get by and even do well by some people's standards, but your ability to have an impact on the world will be significantly reduced. Without goals, you will never be able to harness the true potential of your unique gifts and talents. Your happiness and success may well be more accidental than planned. Are you a gambler? Do you want to gamble your future happiness and well-being?

Without goals, you may drift like a leaf blowing in the wind – aimless and lacking purpose, or direction. Passively accepting life by default rather than assertively choosing your life by design, comparing yourself to others ('compareitis' as I call it) instead of running your own race. By not setting goals and designing your own life plan, you will be much more likely to fall into someone else's plan. And guess what that may mean for you?

Without goals, a sense of self-satisfied complacency and mediocrity can set in. You can develop middle-age spread (of your brain not your tummy), when your brain cells get flabby and lazy because they are not being stretched or challenged enough. Without goals, you may find yourself stuck in a rut, deep in your comfort zone, never challenging yourself to become more than what you are.

Without goals, you may become the self-induced victim of circumstance, and negative thinking patterns. 'Poor me. If only.' Without goals you may stay small in your thinking and may wallow in self-righteous pity. Argue for your limitations and they become your limitations!

Without goals, you do not get the constructive feedback and the accountability you need for sustainable success in life. By taking 100 per cent responsibility for your life, all feedback, both positive and negative, becomes a useful opportunity to either reinforce existing habits or behaviours or to make improvements, to learn and grow.

Have you ever suffered from 'Weekend Syndrome': a work-free day where you wake up with no agenda or no plan of what you are going to do, and drift aimlessly, accomplishing little, and feeling a little guilty when it's over? When you face each day with a plan you can get a lot more done and derive more energy and enjoyment from your activities. Even a very simple plan like exercising, going on a short trip or meeting up with friends allows you to feel so much better in yourself. Your weekend break allows you to feel much more refreshed, recharged and reinvigorated!

Goal Setting – Keys to Success

If you go to an optician for an eye check, they will perform an eyesight test and measure your vision. Perfect vision is often described as 20/20. For me 20/20 vision also represents something else. They say that hindsight is always 20/20 vision but why not foresight? I mean the possibility to set and work towards meaningful goals: specifically twenty goals over the next twenty years, real 20/20 vision!

Michelangelo, the Renaissance sculptor and artist, wrote that 'the greatest danger for most of us in life is not that we aim too high and fail to get there but that we aim too low and get there too easily.' So what are you waiting for? Get your journal or notepad and write down twenty goals, big and small, that you want to achieve over the next twenty years. Allow yourself to dream big; be daring and adventurous, no limits. Have some fun! When setting goals, I believe it can be helpful to remember my '5P's' of Successful Goal Setting:

Plan passionately;

Pursue purposefully;

Proceed positively;

Practise persistently;

Progress patiently.

Here are some time-tested tips to help get you started on this new exciting journey.

Write down the right goals, right now!

The first key to goal setting is to dream up a vision of what you want to achieve and who you want to become. Begin with the end in mind. Write down goals for all the areas that are personally important and interesting in your life and not just your career. These might include health, family, relationships, hobbies, self-development. Remember the importance of balance. Prioritise one goal in each area of your life and even within those, choose one goal as your top priority.

It is so important to write your goals down and to describe them clearly. You must have a written plan. For me this is the most important step, because there is no real commitment until your goal has been written down on paper. If you don't know where you want to get to in life, then you are simply not going to arrive. So write down your goals in your journal. Write them down, write them down, write them down!

Once they are written down, they are out of your head and can now start to take on a life journey of their own. Taking the necessary action steps to help you achieve your goals is so much more likely if you write them down rather than if you just talk and fantasise about them. Keep the main bullet points in an easy to access place like your mobile phone or wallet as well as in your journal. Reading and re-reading your written goals daily helps to keep them prominent in your mind.

Watch your comfort zone

Most of us are creatures of habit and, given a choice, crave the security of what is familiar and known (the comfort zone). Setting effective goals is all about challenging yourself to get out of your comfort zone: far enough to stretch you but, at the same time, not totally unrealistic. Sounds easy, right! If you are like most people, then not only do you not like change, you may actively resist it. Setting big goals may make you feel so uncomfortable you come out in a rash. That's OK! Feel the fear and do it anyway.

And, in my experience, it's so much easier to do this when you are able to fine-tune your psychological fitness, build the right ratio of happy to poison dwarfs and take on board some of the other commitments to expand your happiness. Remember happiness leads to success!

Have the courage to build the knowledge, skills and attitudes that support better choices and new possibilities for your life. Lasting change in your life always starts with change on the inside. By harnessing the power of your subconscious mind, it becomes far more probable that you will achieve goal success.

Think Long Term; Act Now!

You need to plan long term: think about some lifelong or twenty-year goals as well as shorter timeframes like one- or three-year goals. Break these down into smaller ninety-day goals, a weekly planner and your daily habits. Peel it right back. What needs to start happening this month, this week, today to move you forward on the journey towards your goals? Planning ahead in blocks of time of at least a week allows you to begin to build a strategy that maximises the chance of your achieving your goals in different aspects of your health and your life.

The Chinese philosopher Lao Tzu wrote that a journey of a thousand miles begins with a single step. Sometimes, taking that first step towards your goal and simply beginning can be the hardest battle of all. Simply doing something, however small, can diminish doubt, keep you focused, and change how you feel about your goals. The secret to getting started is to break your goals down into smaller sub-goals or bite-sized chunks. In this way you can link your important 20/20 goals back to what you need to do today to move you towards that goal.

Use your journal to answer the following questions: What are the small steps that I need to achieve along the way towards this goal? When will I carry out these actions? Do I need any resources to support me?

Suppose your goal is to improve your physical health by eating more healthily. Your first sub-goal might be to keep a food diary for a week and keep a record of everything you eat and drink during that time to give you a much better picture of your current dietary habits. Your next sub-goal might be to make some small improvements to your shopping by drawing up a list of proper healthful foods to purchase before you go shopping. Next you might decide to eat more fresh vegetables each day, to replace white bread with wholegrain bread, and to drink more water. All of these are important achievable sub-goals that support your bigger goal of improved physical health.

Focus less on knowing and more on being

Being passionately committed

As the saying goes, the road to hell is paved with good intentions; until you are fully committed, there is always the possibility of 'excusitis'. You need to be passionately committed to your goals; you need to own them. This gap between being pleasantly interested as opposed to being passionately committed is what you need to bridge to achieve true success in terms of your goals. Goals may be more likely to succeed if you commit publicly to them. Tell your loved ones, family and work colleagues about your goals; make your journey their journey and everyone becomes invested in a successful outcome.

Being more specific and accountable

Having a vague plan to read more books might be a good idea but making that goal specific by committing to a specific objective to read a book a week, or fifty books in the next year, is much more impactful. Specific goals produce specific results, vague goals produce vague results. When you are setting goals, be as specific as you can; being really clear about your goals and your objectives can set you on the path to achieving them. Making lasting change in your life isn't easy for anyone. It takes time and persistence. Get some people on board to help keep you on track with your goals, people who support your growth as you support theirs.

Being the change

The only person you can change in this world is yourself; it is pointless setting goals to try to change another person or that depend on the help of others for completion. If you want more love in your life, be more loving. If you want more happiness in your life become a happier person. If you want more peace in your life become more peaceful. If you want to achieve bigger goals you need to become a bigger person.

Use your imagination

Imagine what it would be like when you achieve your goals. Visualising your goals on a regular basis can really heighten your awareness of the need to bring the people and resources into your life that can make a difference. Reconnect with your dreams and heartfelt goals; describe them as clearly as possible. Imagine yourself having already achieved your goal. What does this look and feel like? Think about the sounds, smells, tastes and textures. Use your imagination and describe in rich detail how this feels for you. By harnessing the energy of your subconscious mind you can develop crystal-clear clarity, leading to better results in your life.

Once you believe in yourself, the journey towards goal success becomes much more of a possibility. Believe in the talent within you, in your ability and potential to achieve. More importantly, believe in the possibility that you can improve, reach new heights and become a better person because of the action steps you are committed to taking.

Count the cost; anticipate the challenges

Sit down and count the cost of working towards your goals. Are you prepared to do what it takes, to have the laser-like focus and discipline, to give yourself the protected time you need to work on your goal? Bottom line, are you willing to pay the price?

Setting goals can conjure up strong emotion in the form of poison dwarfs, especially Fear. Prepare for the self-doubt, negative self-talk, and inner critic urging you to quit after just a few steps. Writing in your journal can really help here. There are always challenges and choices to be made. Learn to plan for at least some of these 'what if' scenarios ahead of time by looking around the corners and figuring out how you might respond to a specific challenge, situation or person. You can't anticipate everything; there are always unknown unknowns. But proper preparation can turn the tide and tip the scales in your favour. Turn the 'Can I or Can't I, Will I or Won't I'? into the 'When I will, and How?' of goal achievement.

Suppose you set yourself the goal of running a marathon as I did. One obvious challenge is the time commitment of all the training. Devise a concrete plan to help you overcome this challenge – for example you might decide to get up an hour earlier in the morning or cut out an hour of TV in the evening. Become more self-aware and quarantine those negative thoughts. Developing a positive action plan for your goal will strengthen your resolve, boost self-confidence and build your blueprint for goal success.

The little wins are the big wins

If you improve yourself by one per cent each day, what will happen after 100 days? One hundred per cent improvement! Goals are achieved one step at a time. A house is built one brick at a time. A business grows bigger one customer at a time. Taking small steps each and every day towards your goals keeps you moving in the right direction. Just as if you go to the tallest tree in the forest with a sharp axe and you swing five sharp blows with the axe each day, eventually the tree falls down.

It is so important to celebrate the 1 per cent wins; to acknowledge you are on the right track and appreciate the progress you have made. Celebrating brings on the happy dwarfs which will support even more success on your journey. Celebrating your achievements, however small, with those you love and care about is also a very powerful way to build and cement those relationships.

Dead Person's Goals

Unfortunately, many people set goals in negative terms because they are much more aware of what they don't want than what they do want from life. 'Dead Person's Goals' is a term I use for these types of goals that simply involve 'Stop doing this' or 'Stop doing that.' These negatively phrased goals are usually self-defeating because they bring on the poison dwarfs – especially Fear and Anxiety. These guys will dance around in your head and lead you on a self-fulfilling downward spiral where guilt and negativity get to cast their long shadow over you.

Reflecting on and reframing your experiences

What have you learned from this experience? What went well and why? What can go better the next time and how? What is the opportunity to grow here? Reflecting on and learning from your experience and making improvements is a powerful way to live your life and can make the journey of goal achievement much more meaningful.

Reframe your thinking. For example you might ask yourself: 'If I was no longer bingeing on junk food, how could I use my time in a more meaningful way to support improvements in my health?' Answering this in a more positive way can be really helpful. 'Well, maybe I would feel more positive in myself, I would definitely be healthier and it would help me become fitter.' So perhaps a better goal to set than the goal of losing weight might be the goal of becoming healthier by committing to eat more healthily and to take more exercise.

Value your values

Is what you are doing right now taking you closer to or further from the person that you want to become? Suppose you value health and your goal is to exercise daily before you go to work. You wake up one morning early and you do not feel like exercising because you feel tired and it is windy, wet and wintery outside. But you have committed to your goal so you drag yourself out of bed into your running gear and go for your workout anyway. Afterwards you feel terrific, not just from the endorphin release from exercise but because you have achieved your sub-goal of exercise that day. The result is your exercise habit is reinforced, your self-esteem rises, and your character is strengthened.

A goal is something specific that you want to achieve. For example you might set yourself the goal of running the New York Marathon as I have done. So you devise an action plan and set yourself a number of specific sub-goals that allow you to monitor your progress along the way. Once you have run that marathon and the goal is achieved, it is a done deal. However, when your value is health, there is no final destination. The pursuit of improved health is a continuous journey with no destination, so no matter how far you travel, there is always further to go, new understandings to discover. Valuing your health gives you the drive to build on the habit of regular exercise even when you don't feel like it. Connecting with your values helps you to be more resilient, to avoid giving up in the face of adversity, to stop saying it is too hard.

Values give life meaning, passion and purpose. Connecting with your values gives you a sense that what you are doing in life is worth it. So if you value your health you will be willing to commit time to exercise on a regular basis, because you believe it is worth it. So a value is a motivating tool.

Balance

It is so important to balance the writing and planning of goals which is all about your future with taking the time to appreciate what is going well and happening in your life right now and enjoying that for what it is. Balance the journey towards the mountaintop with the daily freedom of being in the moment. Take the time to enjoy the one day that anyone has – today, right here, right now! Take the time to smell the roses. Remember that life is indeed a temporary gift with an unknown expiry date.

Imagine a trampoline and the trampoline has got four support pillars. The first pillar represents your happiness and the health of your emotions. The second pillar represents your psychological fitness: your self-awareness and belief, self-development, self-acceptance. The third pillar represents your physical health: your energy and nutrition, hydration, exercise, rest, lifestyle, and what I call 'health IQ' – your knowledge and awareness, allowing you to make more informed choices and decisions in terms of your long-term health. The fourth pillar represents your relationships, not just with yourself and your loved ones, but also with your work colleagues and your community, the people you can turn to for support and help when you need it.

A PRESCRIPTION FOR HAPPINESS

The membrane of the trampoline represents the 'glue' between the pillars: the fact that all four pillars are interconnected and interdependent. Just as a trampoline needs four strong pillars to function properly so too you need integrated physical, psychological, emotional and relationship 'pillars' for optimal health and well-being.

Weakness in one area of your trampoline will cause imbalance and rebound onto the other areas. If one pillar starts to crack and crumble, your entire trampoline may collapse. The trampoline metaphor symbolises balance: so important for your ability to destress and bounce back. If you just focus intensely on one pillar of your trampoline, this may be detrimental to your overall well-being. Think of all the people who spend all that time working on their careers at the expense of their personal relationships.

Everyone has stuff jumping up and down on their trampoline which reflects the busyness of daily life – commitments, deadlines and responsibilities. Now imagine that a big elephant begins to bounce up and down on your trampoline. This might represent a health crisis, a challenging situation at work or at home, a relationship issue or a sense of loss. Your trampoline starts to creak under the pressure. This is when the pillars of your trampoline need to be strong, so you can be resilient and bounce back. If not, then your trampoline might crack and you will leak vital emotional energy; your health and well-being will suffer.

The best way to make your pillars strong is to set and work towards goals for your relationships as well as your emotional, psychological and physical health. In so doing you can reap the rewards of great relationships, build your psychological and physical fitness and expand your happiness.

By doing this you get to become more of who you are truly meant to be. You can reach more of your potential, and your future bounce can exceed even your wildest expectations.

A PRESCRIPTION FOR HAPPINESS

Small daily improvements!

During that transition when the caterpillar spins his cocoon and morphs into the butterfly, everything changes. By committing to changing the old familiar ways of doing things, you are rigorously rewiring and recalibrating your brain. It's not easy to make sustainable improvements for the better. It takes real courage. What's more, real life can have a habit of blowing you off track. And yet your commitment to persevere, to stay the course on the journey of improvement, is where the greatest opportunities for growth lie. This can be a really emergent time, where something really beautiful is being created. For the caterpillar the end; for the butterfly a beautiful new beginning. As you stretch yourself and get out of your comfort zone, you can shed those old habits and behaviours that no longer serve your purpose and transform yourself with confidence and boldness. And those small, daily, seemingly insignificant improvements can make a big difference.

You might think that to achieve major goals you have to make big changes, but that is not the case. In fact small changes can lead to seismic results! One of Newton's laws will tell you that every action has an equal and opposite reaction. However, Edward Lorenz, a brilliant meteorologist, showed through the study of the variables that impact on weather, that small changes in weather in one part of the world could have major impacts on weather systems elsewhere - the so-called 'butterfly effect'. In his seminal paper he posed the question: 'Does the Flap of a Butterfly's Wing in Brazil Set Off a Tornado in Texas?' In his book *The Essence of Chaos,* Lorenz highlights how precise rules may govern apparently random behaviour. The butterfly principle illustrates beautifully how small changes can have unforeseen consequences, and lead to seismic results, unforeseeable along the traditional lines of cause and effect. This butterfly principle turned on its head the long-held view that the universe was a large machine in which causes matched effects and was the beginning of 'chaos theory', one of the major scientific breakthroughs of the twentieth century. The bottom line is that small changes can make a big difference when it comes to working towards your goals, transforming your life, and expanding your happiness. What is the one thing you can do, starting today, that can move you in the direction of the person you want to become?

The Fifth Commitment:

Making Time – For What Matters

Modern healthcare is weighed down with data, numbers and statistics. With the growing obesity epidemic in the western world, weight and expanding waistlines have become a big issue. In my experience as a doctor, so many people get up on the weighing scales and, as a result, feel negatively about themselves. Weighing yourself can be a great way to bring on some of the poison dwarfs, especially Guilt! In recent years it has been realised that fat stores are perhaps even more important than weight per se. And perhaps the best and simplest way to measure belly fat, especially in men, is with a tape measure. Actions speak louder than words so while the weighing scales was removed from my consulting room, the tape measure became one of my best friends, professionally speaking!

One day after a medical assessment, my patient John and I were discussing goal setting in terms of his health and well-

being. The tape measure was on the desk so I picked it up and, giving him a scissors, asked him to cut the tape measure at his current age (forty-four years old). About half of the tape measure fell away. Next I asked him to make a second cut at the number he expected to live to – he chose eighty-five years! Next I asked him to cut off a further third, given that he will spend a third of his life sleeping. With surprise he held the greatly diminished piece of tape. I gently said, 'John, that's all the time you have left. To dream your dreams and do those things you know are most important.' Tears welled up in his eyes as the slow realisation of his limited time dawned on him. I encouraged him to use his journal to reassess his priorities and to ask himself the challenging questions: deep down what did he really, really want for his life?

The next time I met John, almost two years later, he was beaming and radiating contentment. He said so much had changed for him since we had met last. When I explored this in depth with him, it transpired that the tape measure experience had been a major wake-up call for him. He realised he was spending too much of his free time with the wrong people, living in the past, and had never learned to let go of previous life failures. He had found himself somewhat drifting through life, stuck in the comfort zone, wallowing in 'excusitis' and enduring the pain of regret rather than experiencing the pain of discipline and the freedom it ultimately brings. For the first time ever, he had written down his goals, not the usual endless list of business goals but goals for his relationships, his family and their future together. By taking complete responsibility for the life changes he needed to make, he stopped resisting change and instead embraced change with a renewed sense of purpose

He had taken his family to China to see the Great Wall and to fulfil a childhood dream of experiencing close up the black and white panda bears in their natural environment. And closer to home, he had rekindled his love of reading, something he had first learned from his grandmother as a young boy, but had let go of for so many years. He had also discovered the happiness benefits of volunteering by giving some time for a community fundraising effort.

'Lives of great men all remind us

We can make our lives sublime,

And, departing, leave behind us

Footprints on the sands of time.'
Henry Longfellow.

Do what you love, love what you do

I think of time as the marker of the past, the keeper of the present, and the dreamer of the future. Like grains of sand slipping through your fingers, time is a scarce commodity that everyone wants more of. Benjamin Franklin once wrote that 'Lost time is never found again.' So true! A life of ninety years has only 1,080 months, about 32,850 days or 788,400 hours. And that's it – time up! The average human life is short, often far too short not to dream your dreams, face the truth of your life for what it is and live at your highest potential.

What you do with your time matters; it is not as important to count time as it is to make time count. Many people spend so much valuable time and energy simply being busy at the expense of building their health and expanding their happiness.

This is the natural tension in life between what I term your clock and your compass. The clock is a reminder of the urgent deadlines, timetables and responsibilities. The clock: that great destroyer of time. The compass represents your vision, values, and the overall direction of your life. It's a reminder of what's most important: what, deep down, you really, really want. Which is why it is important to be mindful, not just of the clock, but of the moral compass in your life. Goethe, the philosopher, once wrote that those things that matter most should never be at the price of those things that matter least.

Your relationship with time includes managing yourself and your priorities and making sure you are doing the right things as opposed to just doing things right. To become more effective, consider planning your time in terms of weekly chunks. Schedule some protected time at the weekend, say Sunday morning, to sit down and plan the next seven days, making sure to mark in time for those things that are important to you (for example family, health, key relationships). Having the discipline to do this better enables you to prioritise what's important and to develop more life perspective; it ensures you will not be displaced or distracted by needless negativity or by things that are neither urgent nor important.

There are no magic pills to enhanced enjoyment from a fast-paced life. The key is to slow down and simplify; to do less but be more effective; experience more of the moments. Use your journal to reflect and explore what you really, really want from life. Develop the freedom to say yes to those things that matter most to you and the courage to say no to the rest.

You have your own unique strengths, talents and abilities which help to make you the person you are. Learning to focus on your strengths might sound corny but the reality is that most people tend to focus on their faults and weaknesses. Modern society focuses on your flaws, and why you need to fix them – from plastic surgery, to being a size zero. The key is to stop worrying about weakness so much and start using your strengths. A strengths-based approach to your happiness will make you psychologically stronger, allowing you to do more and be more. So change your thinking to a more strength-based mind sight. Develop more awareness, clarity and insight into your innate strengths and abilities; understand what they are, and how to use them more effectively to support you in expanding your happiness.

Martin Seligman and Chris Peterson undertook a brilliant, in-depth, analysis of wisdom books down through the ages, from the writings of Aristotle and Confucius to the Bible, the Bhagavadgita and the Koran. They discovered that there appear to be six core characteristics or virtues common to every culture and religion. These core virtues are courage, justice, love, wisdom, temperance and transcendence, and they have been further subdivided into twenty-four character strengths. From this work, Seligman and Peterson have developed a VIA Signature Strengths Questionnaire (available free online at www.authentichappiness.org), through which you can identify your signature strengths (strengths that you most readily identify with, that energise and excite you when using them, that feel part of the real you).

Strengths are empowering for your happy dwarfs and elevating for those around you. While learning about your strengths can give you a temporary boost in your well-being, using your signature strengths regularly in your life can significantly expand your happiness and lower feelings of depression. Many people know all about their weaknesses but don't know what their signature strengths are. To reap the many benefits of playing from your strengths, including the possibility of expanding your happiness and performing better, you need to firstly know what these strengths are and then learn to apply them in meaningful ways.

Imagine a sailboat on the ocean which has a big sail and a leak; this leak (signifying your weaknesses) has to be plugged so the boat doesn't sink. However if you focus all your time, energy and attention on the leak (and your weaknesses), then you are never going to get anywhere. Your big sail represents your strengths and it is only by giving energy and attention to your strengths that you are going to be able to cross the ocean of possibility in your life. This is a journey worth taking: the journey of self-discovery, of self-exploration, of mastery.

Some strengths have been shown to be particularly closely linked with your happiness and well-being. These include gratitude, hope (realistic optimism), love, curiosity, enthusiasm, and, of course, the power of strong interpersonal relationships. For example, the strength of curiosity encourages you to explore what's novel about any situation, leading to new discoveries and personal growth. To build your strength of curiosity, you might decide to read an article or watch a documentary about something you know nothing about. You might talk to unusual people, expose yourself to new experiences and try new things.

What are your best skills, talents and strengths? What are your signature strengths? Use your journal to explore which of your strengths allows you to become more fully alive. Which parts of your life allow you to use more of your signature strengths? Which parts drain you of your strengths? How can you redesign your life so that you can better use your own signature strengths? What changes might you need to make so that you can devote more time and energy to those things that you do best?

In the Zone, Finding Flow

The concept of 'flow' has been extensively described by a brilliant Russian psychologist Mihaly Csikszentmihalyi, (pronounced chick-sent-me-high) in his book *Flow: The Psychology of Optimal Experience*. His work on flow originally studied artists, with their intense focus and steely concentration, often for hours at a time, as they became totally immersed in the process of painting. He described their joy at doing something simply for the sheer sake of it: the journey of creating art in the moment, not the destination or final product.

Having interviewed thousands of people from many different backgrounds, he has shown that creating flow experiences in your life can be the gateway to happiness, at the very heart of a flourishing life. Flow is a universal psychological experience characterised by being creative, happy and energised: being stretched to the very limit trying to achieve something worthwhile. You are motivated for personal growth; the challenges are high but well matched by your skills and abilities. You are so engaged and absorbed in what you are doing that it becomes a state of effortless concentration and enjoyment. You are in the zone: fully engaged, the activity intrinsically rewarding, its own reward.

You experience pleasure while performing at, or close to, the best of your ability – peak experience through peak performance. Creating more opportunities to achieve more of your human potential allows you to enter flow states with happiness ensuing as a result. While twenty per cent of people regularly enter flow states, unfortunately, Csikszentmihalyi, has found that fifteen per cent never do. This is a great pity because flow is the fulfilment of your purpose, the best use of your own unique gifts and talents. As your life becomes more in flow, you become more playful, creative and authentic. Just as the spirit of gratitude is learning to want what you have, the essence of flow is being in the moment, where action and awareness are merged.

Imagine you are out of your comfort zone being stretched by some task (good stress) which is challenging and requires skill. You know that you have the right skills to deal with the challenges posed and you are concentrating fully. You have a clear sense of control over what you are doing: clear goals, lots of sub-goals, every step of your journey mapped out. You have immediate feedback on your performance and you have a good chance of completing it.

With flow, there is no fear of failure, only a deep feeling

of enjoyment. You are so focused on what you are doing, free from the concerns or competing interests of everyday life, that your self-consciousness disappears. However, after a flow experience, your sense of self is strengthened and you become more than you were before. Your sense of time is altered: hours can pass by in minutes, and minutes can stretch out to seem like hours.

Creating flow experiences in your life can be a silver bullet for expanding your happiness and optimising your experience of life itself. Flow experiences can give you a deep sense of enjoyment and total engagement with life.

Imagine that life is like a river. One bank represents boredom, the other anxiety. In life, many people are clinging to the river bank, afraid to let go. But when you have the courage to let go and go with the flow there is a wonderful sense of liberation. This is where you follow the spirit of the Tao: 'going with the flow'. One of the keys to an emotionally rich life is to learn to create flow experiences everywhere, to really live and be in the moment.

Flow experiences can build your sense of realistic optimism and allow you to deal more positively with the inevitable challenges that life throws your way. When those challenges are too low in relation to your skills you may feel bored; too high and you tend to feel anxious and frustrated. Flow experiences allow you to better navigate the river of life between those twin pillars of boredom and anxiety. Flow represents optimal balance between your perceived abilities and the perceived challenge of the task at hand – when there is neither boredom (too much skill for the challenge) nor anxiety (too much challenge for the skill).

Flow experiences strengthen your psychological fitness and support your personal growth and development. You become more receptive to new experiences, more committed to learning new things.

Common sources of flow experiences for many people include driving the car, meaningful work where you use your talents or strengths, talking to friends, cooking a good meal, gardening, studying. For me, I find one of the best ways to enter flow is teaching about health leadership and well-being: stretching me to support others in making improvements in their lives.

Pursue your passionate purpose in life with passion, purpose and persistence; do what you love, and love what you do. If you love what you do, you will bring a level of enthusiasm and positive energy to bear that's next to impossible to match through sheer effort alone. Be more curious and interested in the world around you; open up to new and different opportunities and experiences. Be challenged by everyday activities in your life; stretch yourself and keep on learning. Move from simply turning up to turning it on, from autopilot to full engagement.

To create more flow experiences in your life become more flow-like in your outlook and become self-aware enough to pay attention to what is going on around you. Use your journal to explore those times you lose yourself in an activity that uses your skills and leaves you feeling energised afterwards. Use your journal to know yourself better and those activities that allow you to enter into flow.

Happiness at work – Hi ho, hi ho, it's off to work we go!

The City and Guilds' Happiness League Tables in the UK have found that among the happiest workers are florists and gardeners. Perhaps it is the timeless connection with nature, creating beauty for others, a strong sense of meaning. Perhaps they find their work to be pleasurable and it allows them to use their strengths as a person. Perhaps it is the sense of sowing seeds and reaping the rewards; perhaps being a florist or gardener is simply good fun! Groundbreaking research by the Gallup Organisation in 1958 found that among men who lived to the ripe old age of ninety-five, the average retirement age was eighty. What kept them working for such a long time? For the vast majority (93 per cent) it was meaningful work, with 86 per cent finding their work to be fun. This level of work engagement makes you more committed and connected; caring about your job is really good for your long-term health and vitality.

It's well recognised that the most important investment any organisation can make is in its people. Happiness and well-being in the workplace impact on overall life satisfaction, just as overall happiness in life tends to spill over to expand happiness at work.

Any mention of workplace happiness has to start with the happiness and positivity of the leadership team. Because of the highly contagious nature of both positive and negative emotion, leadership culture and style can impact significantly on the well-being of the entire organisation. Furthermore the degree of positivity within an organisation also matters, big time! Brilliant research by leading positive psychologist, Barbara Fredrickson, has found that organisations which flourish have a tipping point of positivity to negativity of at least 3:1. She has described in her book, *Positivity*, how once this ratio was reached, key performance indicators in organisations from profitability to customer satisfaction improved.

Happier workers tend to make better work colleagues, and are more sociable with less interpersonal work conflict. They are more resourceful and resilient, with higher job engagement and enjoyment, less burnout and fewer sick days. Moreover, they tend to have higher quality of work, more career success, even higher incomes! In fact, higher income may well be more related to your happiness than educational achievement; happier people tend to form better relationships and have higher emotional intelligence.

There is a growing number of people who are dissatisfied nowadays in the world of work. While there may be many reasons for this sense of discontent, the relentless focus on the bottom line, bigger profit margins, and pursuit of ever more productivity can often be at the expense of the personal well-being of the employees. A win-lose, rather than win-win! Feeling supported at work and strong work relationships are key factors in employee satisfaction, not surprising given that positive psychology has found that robust relationships are probably the leading indicator of your overall well-being. Given the highly interdependent nature of modern workplaces, looking on your work relationships as real investments can reap significant dividends, not just for your individual happiness, but for the overall success and well-being of the organisation.

While not every job is a bed of roses, the one thing each person can control, irrespective of their work environment, is their own attitude to work. 'Before Enlightenment, chop wood, carry water. After Enlightenment, chop wood, carry water': this Zen saying highlights, for me, the fundamental importance that meaningful work plays in life. Not surprisingly, losing your job and unemployment can trigger unhappiness and result in a significant decrease in life satisfaction.

Amy Wrzesniewski (pronounced rez-NES-kee) of Yale

A PRESCRIPTION FOR HAPPINESS

University has carried out some fascinating research on how your job performance can be influenced and affected by your belief systems. She has found that people have one of three mind sights about their work: seeing it as a job, a career or a calling. And it appears to be about one third in each category, irrespective of the type of job: professor or plumber, doctor or driver, waiter or Wall-Street banker.

For those people who see their work simply as a job, it's perceived as a chore to be suffered with the sole emphasis on the pay cheque. The work itself is done because they have to do it; however it may provide very little fulfilment or interest for them beyond it being a means to an end. This can be a recipe for major work dissatisfaction and disillusionment, particularly if you believe you are not being fairly compensated for your efforts. By seeing your work as a career, you may still work because you have to – but you are much more likely to be personally invested in the work, and want to succeed. The rewards are seen as being mainly external: prestige, power, and position. Once promotions and recognition cease you may start to become dissatisfied – and lose interest altogether.

If you see your work as a calling, you work for the sake of the work itself. You probably love your work, to the extent that you would keep doing it even for free if you could afford to. Because you see your work as being meaningful, having a higher purpose and making a positive contribution to the world, you are happy to work for the sake of the work itself. The real rewards are internal for you as you get to use your strengths to provide you with purpose and meaning. As you are more invested in this calling type of work, you will persist and persevere longer and be more likely to succeed as a result. Workers that see their work as a calling, or vocation, have much higher job satisfaction and overall life satisfaction than people who simply see their job in terms of clocking in or out and collecting the pay cheque. And seeing your work as a calling depends not on your job title or office size, nor job-spec or pay cheque, but simply on the degree of meaning you choose to find in your work.

Because meaning is created by you, as an individual person, rather than by your job title, you can turn up the 'meaning sensometer' in your job (indeed in any job), as the human mind is a meaning-making machine! Just as there are some doctors and lawyers who simply see their work as a job, so there are street cleaners who see their work as a calling. By reframing your mind sight and recrafting your job description more as a calling, you can focus on ways to derive more meaning from what you do and create greater happiness at work. A useful way to do this is to downplay the monetary aspects of the job and instead focus on the ways in which you get to use more of your signature strengths and serve and support others. Ask yourself in what ways does your work provide meaning and benefit others?

The helicopter, tank, submarine and scuba gear are just some of the products of Leonardo Da Vinci's creativity and imagination, described in detail in the *Codex Atlanticus*, a twelve-volume, thousand-page exposé of his brilliance. This extraordinarily brilliant artist, inventor and ultimate Renaissance man so accurately predicted so many advancements in science, medicine and warfare five hundred years before they happened! Could he have achieved all of that without the courage to dream big and be really creative?

Creativity in the workplace is so important to foster innovation, yet deadlines, time pressures and a sense of urgency can hamper the very creativity that's most needed; working too hard can sometimes hinder, not help, long-term success. Teresa Amabile, in the Harvard Business Review, has described how time-pressured environments can foster frustration, feelings of negativity, and a narrowing range of thinking and creativity – unless there is the ability to become immersed in a project, giving it undivided attention with clear focus, free from distractions.

A phrase commonly used by people in the well-being space is the expression 'work-life balance'; to me this makes little sense given the tremendous potential health and happiness benefits of meaningful work. In fact you could argue that work-life balance is only applicable to work that is perceived to be a chore or possibly some career work. And the key word here is 'perceive': no matter what your job, how you choose to perceive it is up to you! For me the only balance that matters is the balance between positive and negative emotion (the happy and poison dwarfs at or above 3:1) for you as a person, as well as in your organisation – to support you in flourishing and being at your very best, whether at work, rest or play.

The Sixth Commitment:

Exercise – The Greatest Pill of All

When I (first) saw him Michael – let's call him that – was a heart attack waiting to happen. Aged only forty-one, years of poor eating habits and a sedentary lifestyle coupled with a bad family history and recent stress had led to chest pain and a late night trip to hospital. The diagnosis: heart disease, narrowed coronary arteries and damage to his heart muscle confirmed by tests. Without a major overhaul in lifestyle, the next step would be bypass surgery or worse! He could hardly climb the stairs in his own house without feeling out of breath. His belly measured 46 inches while both blood pressure and cholesterol were raised. He was so scared, terrified even, and let go of his usual male bravado. He had a wife and adorable young children. He had so much to lose and he knew it. Better still, he wanted to do something about his health, to change his ways, to make a difference. Bottom line: he wasn't going to give up. His health crisis became the bedrock on which he rebuilt his health and his life.

With support and gentle encouragement, Michael turned things around. Using his journal, he was able to set and achieve small baby goals. Step by step, day by day, he built the habits of moving more and eating better. I gave him the ambitious target of walking the half-marathon – and six months later he did. A year later he walked a full marathon! By embracing the game-changing benefits of exercise, Michael has totally transformed his health and his life.

Epictetus, the philosopher, has highlighted that your attitude is the one thing you can control in life, not what other people think or do or say. Time and again over the years, I've encountered people who, with the right attitude, simply refuse to allow the label of an illness to define who they are or what they are about. These are the people who consistently do better when faced with the adversity of life's inevitable challenges.

As a long-time believer in the benefits of exercise, I have always enjoyed a regular game of tennis, a run on the beach or a kick around. Personally, I can't imagine trying to deal with the challenges of life without the stress-busting benefits of regular exercise; what's more, it can be great fun staying in good shape. But on reflection, my life has been punctuated with 'off spells': not exercising for several weeks at a time, particularly in the depths of those depressingly bleak Irish winters. 'Excusitis' takes many forms and along with being 'too busy', the Irish weather was one of mine. Every New Year, high on my list of resolutions would be to take more exercise. Deep down I knew how much better exercise made me feel; I knew what I should do but didn't seem to understand how to make exercise an integral part of my daily routine.

Thanks to my exploration of philosophy and evidence-based positive psychology, I discovered the power of keeping a journal. Now I could record my exercise habits and review them on a weekly basis. Partly as a record of what I had done, but, more importantly, in order to understand the 'why', especially those days when things had not worked out as planned. Learning from my experiences in this way and connecting what I was thinking and feeling to what I was doing was an 'aha moment'. A whole new level of self-understanding began to open up which allowed me to see my commitment to health improvement as much more of a long-term journey with no end point in sight.

Now I have been able to commit to the habit of daily exercise (OK so I miss the odd day still, and sometimes take a rest day and that's OK too). For me the habit of regularity has been instrumental in me bedding exercise down as a habit. This meant that instead of vaguely committing to exercise more often at some time in the future, I was making the specific commitment to exercise every day (including today). This was a game changer for me. All those extra happy hormones like serotonin, stress-busting endorphins and motivational boosters like dopamine, all combining to boost my energy and emotional vitality. The result is feeling better, more positive and alive.

I learned from my experience that the best way for me to take more exercise, or make any positive life change, is by building an unbreakable habit. It was so much easier now to keep going than to stop. What had happened was that a new pattern had been hardwired into my brain circuitry. Now I find it hard to imagine a day without some form of physical activity, even if it's just a nice walk by the beach. And the symptoms of withdrawal: noticing an acute sense of discomfort if I missed out on exercise for more than a couple of days. Exercise can be addictive, but a good addiction, the greatest pill of all.

The Greatest Pill of All

Exercise can have remarkable benefits for your health and greatly enhance your sense of well-being. It's a great way to feel fitter and stay younger looking. Regular exercise gives you an energy boost and builds your endurance and stamina, so you can quite simply do more. Being physically active helps you live longer, lowering your risk of premature death. Are you worried about heart disease? Exercise strengthens the heart muscle, and a stronger heart can pump more blood with less effort, reducing the risk of heart attack and stroke. If you already have heart disease, then an exercise programme can significantly reduce your chance of having another heart attack. Regular exercise lowers blood pressure and tends to thin the blood, making it less likely to clot.

Exercise helps to stimulate the metabolism (the rate at which your body burns calories and fat), not just during exercise but for some time afterwards. Your body gets turned into more of a fat-burning machine. So exercise helps maintain weight loss and prevents excess weight gain and obesity. Exercise helps lower total cholesterol levels, raise the HDL (good) cholesterol level, lower the LDL (bad) cholesterol level and also helps to lower the blood fat (triglycerides) level by helping your metabolism to burn fat.

Regular exercise reduces the risk of developing diabetes. In people with existing diabetes, regular exercise significantly reduces the risk of complications. Exercise helps strengthen your muscles, reduce body fat and protect against falls. Exercise can reduce the risk of developing several types of cancer and lower your risk of getting gallstones. Exercise can help prevent fractures caused by thinning of the bones (osteoporosis). Regular weight-bearing exercise promotes bone formation and delays bone loss. Regular exercise can help spark up your sex life, protecting men against erectile dysfunction and helping women with arousal. Exercise can boost the immune system, keeping you strong and free from colds and flus. Regular exercise can help promote good restful sleep. However, it is best to avoid heavy exercise late at night as this can leave you too buzzed up to sleep! Exercise also helps protect against the ageing process itself. There can be a huge difference between your age as determined by your date of birth and your biological age (the miles on your clock). Exercise is the one pill I think almost everybody would take if it was freely available in tablet form.

Regular exercise has been shown to be a powerful ally for your psychological fitness, allowing you to think better and more clearly. It is a great natural stress buster, a brilliant way to blow off steam. Exercise reduces levels of the body's stress hormones, like cortisol and adrenaline, and is a powerful way to ward off anxiety and feelings of depression. Exercise is a low-level form of stress itself and regular exercise builds up immunity to this low-level stress, giving you added protection against life's other stressors. Exercise stimulates the production of a number of brain endorphins (natural painkillers that bring on the runner's high) that help you feel calm, optimistic and energised. They minimise feelings of pain or discomfort associated with exercise. These endorphins also produce a positive feeling in the body, even a feeling of euphoria, similar to that of morphine.

Exercising regularly helps you to feel better about yourself, boosting your mood and self-esteem. As you feel and look better, your self-image will improve and persisting with your exercise habit will give you more self-belief, self-mastery and self-confidence. This confidence will spill over into other areas of your life, helping you to work towards other important goals.

Exercise causes the brain to release a substance called BDNF (brain-derived neurotrophic factor), which is like Miracle-Gro for the brain. It acts like a reset button on stress, protecting the brain against stress and helping to repair and replace brain cells. The development of new brain cells is known as neurogenesis and occurs in the brain's learning centre (the hippocampus), which is involved in creating and retrieving memories. By increasing the blood flow to the brain, new pathways are created between brain cells in a process called neuroplasticity which helps your brain to learn and retain new information. Through the stimulation and creation of new neural pathways, exercise can help protect your brain against memory loss or cognitive decline as you get older.

Exercise stimulates the release of brain chemicals like serotonin, the 'happy hormone', a deficiency of which is associated with symptoms of flatness, anxiety and depression. Indeed, exercise is probably one of nature's best natural antidepressants. Exercise boosts dopamine levels in the brain which enhances motivation to get out in the world and do things, resulting in a greater sense of accomplishment. So exercising regularly will make you even more motivated to keep going!

Regular exercise can be a great way to connect with friends in a fun setting, make new friends, and build existing relationships through cultivating shared interests. Friends can also be a great motivational support to encourage you to keep going on an exercise programme – you become your associations! Strong social support is very helpful for people suffering from depression: a real win-win, taking exercise and boosting friendships.

Taking exercise can cultivate feelings of happiness and well-being. You can become more perceptive of what's going on around you: more self-confident with a more positive body image. Exercise can be great fun, engaging in enjoyable activity that can diminish the poison dwarfs, especially Anger, Fear and Anxiety. It can be so good: you might consider it as an 'anti-anxiety vaccine', bringing on the happy dwarfs and giving you that 'zip-a-dee-doo-dah' feeling! To get the most happiness-boosting effects from exercise, you need to exercise daily even if it's only for a short time like twenty minutes.

A PRESCRIPTION FOR HAPPINESS

Getting Your Head around Exercise

Aerobic exercise is exercise that causes the heart to beat faster, improving oxygen consumption in the body. Many of the health benefits from exercise are gained through aerobic exercise. Even simple walking for thirty to forty-five minutes provides excellent health benefits, even at low intensity. However, the heart is a muscle and a pump that strengthens with more vigorous exercise, especially when the heart rate increases to a target heart rate (the rate at which the body is thought to be exercising at its optimum). Once you are comfortable checking your own pulse, you can then check it during exercise to see if you are at your target heart rate. This can be quite easily done by feeling your pulse at your wrist beside your thumb or at your neck under the side of your jaw. If you are unsure or not confident about this, your family doctor will be happy to assist you. By counting your pulse for ten seconds and then multiplying the answer by six you will know what your heart rate is per minute. An average resting heart rate is about seventy beats per minute and people who are fitter tend to have lower resting rates.

This target heart rate is generally 70–85 per cent of your age-adjusted maximum heart rate, which is calculated by the following formula:

220 – Your Age (in years) = Maximum Heart Rate

So, for example, a forty-year-old person's maximum heart rate is calculated accordingly:

Maximum Heart Rate = 220 – 40 = 180 beats per minute.

The target heart rate for aerobic exercise purposes is 70–85 per cent of 180, giving a range from 126–153 beats per minute.

Checking your heart rate is a good way to ensure that you are exercising at your target heart rate and that you are not overdoing it. If you do this type of exercise through cycling, swimming or even brisk walking, for at least thirty minutes four times per week, there are significant health benefits. On the other two or three days of the week, going for a good walk is a great way of stretching your leg muscles and is a more relaxing form of exercise than the heavier aerobic type. If you feel like trying something different, consider Zumba, a highly energetic dance and aerobic fitness programme first created by Columbian dancers. It includes music with fast and slow rhythms and resistance training for all age groups.

High-intensity interval training, or HIIT as it is often called, is a new way to exercise aerobically. As well as boosting aerobic fitness, exercising at high intensity appears to produce a significant afterburn for many hours, meaning you will burn more calories, accelerating fat loss as well as suppressing appetite.

Here the emphasis is all about pushing yourself to your limit, for a very short period of time. We're talking seconds, not minutes! The secret is effort rather than speed. For example you might warm up on an exercise bike for a couple of minutes and then pedal flat out against resistance for six seconds, and then ease off, before repeating the pattern. Running up a few flights of stairs at work can be a great opportunity for HIIT as well. By using gravity for resistance, running upstairs means that you are far less likely to strain or pull a muscle than if you run on the flat. Repeating this pattern a number of times means the exercise programme is over in less than ten minutes. Sometimes less can be more!

For most people, most of the time, exercise is very safe and only good for your health. By following the six sensible steps listed below you can minimise the risks of any health-related problems connected with exercise.

Six Sensible Steps for Safer Exercise

1. **Safety first. Have a medical check-up before you begin a moderately vigorous exercise programme. Your doctor**

can help you tailor your exercise programme to your specific requirements.

2. Listen to your body. Don't exercise if you have a high temperature or feel unwell. If you get short of breath or develop chest pain, dizziness or palpitations during exercise, stop and seek medical attention.

3. Start low and go slow. This is particularly important if you haven't been used to taking exercise. Over a few weeks, gradually increase both the intensity and duration of exercise. This gives your body a chance to get used to the new regime and minimises the risk of injury. Wear proper footwear.

4. Warm up and stretch before and particularly after exercise. Flexibility helps to prevent stiffness and injury.

5. Don't eat for 2 hours before intense exercise.

6. Stay hydrated and remember to drink plenty of fluids. Keeping well hydrated before, during and after exercise is very important to prevent cramp and injury as well as helping to optimise performance and improve recovery afterwards. Remember, thirst is a very poor indicator of hydration and by the time you feel thirsty you may already be quite dehydrated.

Weight Training

Weight training is very important for keeping your muscles and bones strong and healthy. It will benefit people of all ages and athletic abilities. As you get older, this becomes particularly important for body strength, which tends to naturally decline with age. It is estimated that you will lose between five to seven pounds of lean muscle each decade as you age. So weight training can preserve and enhance physical health, help prevent falls and improve quality of life. Body-building, per se, is not the aim. Two or three fifteen-minute sessions, spaced out during the week, are ideal. Using weights can be very good for toning your body, keeping your muscles strong and helping to convert fat to muscle. This, in turn, helps boost your metabolism and burn calories – including sugar and fat – much more efficiently. Doing some light weights also helps protect your joints against wear and tear, strengthens your bones against osteoporosis and boosts energy and stamina.

Put the emphasis on doing comfortable repetitions of low weights rather than going for broke on the Olympic bar. Start low and go slow! Press-ups are an excellent exercise for upper body strength. As with other forms of exercise, it is important not to overdo it. Listen to your own body and know the difference between a little bit of exercise-induced stiffness and the soreness that can come from an injury.

Flexibility Exercises

Stretching should be an essential part of any exercise programme, as it helps to prevent injury and keep the body loose. Working on your flexibility is also an important part of any rehabilitation programme after an injury. Exercises to strengthen the lower back and stomach muscles, often called core stabilisation exercises, are now recognised as being key to injury prevention. Stretching is also a great way to relax and unwind. The growing appreciation of mind-body-soul interface can be seen by the increasing popularity of more holistic forms of exercise such as yoga, pilates and tai chi; all of which have significant health benefits.

Yoga

Yoga teaches that your true nature as a human being and your human potential is not only unknown but unknowable and transcends your sense of self. An ancient art which originated in India, yoga is the practical application of Vedic science, a comprehensive systemic Indian philosophy, going back over 5,000 years. The word yoga is derived from the Sanskrit root yuj, which means 'to unite', which indicates that the purpose of yoga is to unite yourself with your highest nature. Yoga promotes unity of mind, body and spirit and can be practised by anyone regardless of age, experience, body type or physical ability. The very essence of yoga is balance, not just physical balance (range of movement) but balance between body and mind and between mind and spirit.

Yoga requires focused breathing. It teaches that the breath signifies vital energy: that controlling your breathing can also help you control your body and still your mind. Yoga takes concentrated effort and the discipline, drive and determination to practise a series of movements and postures designed to increase the strength, flexibility and fitness of the whole body.

Yoga can be a wonderful way to grow physically, emotionally and psychologically.

Yoga builds emotional vitality and balance in your body and has powerful techniques to create a sense of inner peace, harmony, and clarity of mind. It can help many chronic health conditions including pain, anxiety and depression. It can reduce stress, enhance your mood and expand the sense of creativity and joy in your life. In addition, psychological fitness is strengthened by providing mental clarity and focus. Yoga is a great way to meditate and gain peace of mind, to feel stronger and younger.

Pilates

Pilates is an exercise programme that works on strengthening and developing the entire body to improve balance, muscle-strength, flexibility and good breathing technique. It is a low-impact form of exercise and injuries are uncommon. As well as strong abs or core strength, pilates can support improvements in posture, muscle tone and joint mobility, as well as relieving stress and tension.

Pilates also helps you to develop mind/body connections which increase your awareness of your body. So while pilates incorporates elements of yoga, the main difference between the two is that yoga has a more integrated approach to mind, body and spirit.

Tai Chi

Originating in Chinese philosophy as a martial art, this mind/body practice has considerable health benefits and can be adapted for everyone. Tai chi is thought to unblock and enable the flow of qi (an energy force thought to flow through the body). Tai chi is said to promote balance and harmony between yin and yang, opposing universal elements that need to be kept in unison.

The practice of tai chi integrates the body and mind through three key components. Firstly, *breathing that is regular, really focused and rhythmical, encouraging real relaxation.* Secondly, *slow, steady and structured, low-impact movements* which focus on improving balance, flexibility and coordination as well as posture, alignment and strength. The movements are usually circular and never forced – a series of continuous slow-motion movements. Thirdly, *a meditative state of mind* during tai chi helps to de-stress and to build psychological fitness and emotional vitality. It has been called 'meditation in motion'. Proprioception, the ability to sense the position of one's body, naturally declines with age and tai chi helps this as well as flexibility and balance. Research has shown the benefits of tai chi in helping to prevent falls in patients with Parkinson's Disease and has also demonstrated benefits for a variety of other medical conditions.

Qigong (pronounced cheegong)

This is a close cousin of tai chi but is different in that it's not based on martial arts. A Chinese health practice with roots in traditional Chinese medicine, it is a practice that cultivates qi or life energy. It encompasses gentle repetitive movements, gentle breathing and focused awareness through meditation. This technique may support balance and posture and boosts psychological fitness.

Along with tai chi, it is thought to boost alpha waves in the brain suggesting relaxation and beta waves indicating focus and sharpening of the mind.

Massage

Massage can be a very beneficial way to unwind, relax and recharge. It can help revitalise tired bodies, rejuvenate, and help reduce muscle tension and pain. Massage therapy can improve circulation, and flexibility, and promote deeper breathing. It can help the removal of toxins from the body and help the flow of energy. Psychological fitness is supported by enhanced mental alertness and self-awareness. Massage is a great way to put the Anxiety dwarf back in his box and enhance feelings of peace and well-being. Consider a regular therapeutic massage as part of your holistic well-being programme.

Green Exercise – the great happiness benefits of gardening!

Gardening can be a great form of physical exercise, burning those extra calories and helping you to sleep better, and is really restorative for your psychological fitness and emotional well-being. There's an old Chinese proverb which says if you would be happy all your life, plant a garden! As I reflect on my own love of gardens and nature, I can appreciate how it encourages you to slow down, find yourself and be more in the moment.

Gardening also builds your resilience and sense of realistic optimism. No matter how harsh a winter, there is always next year to look forward to! And what would any self-respecting gardener do with his time if there were no more weeds to sort out! Spending time connecting with nature and the greenery of the natural environment is so relaxing, engaging all your senses in a variety of ways, and so enhancing for your well-being. You get to appreciate the physical presence of nature, notice the seasons and nurture something, the joy of seeing something grow and develop over time. The sense of tending to a garden, minding it and subsequently passing it on to future generations, the reward that comes from reaping the harvest of your own fruit and vegetable patch, no matter how small it may be. Gardening can be a great way to build relationships and strengthen communities. Here in Ireland, the GIY (Grow It Yourself) movement has gained real momentum as a new paradigm for sustainable gardening.

Cicero, the Roman philosopher, wrote about connecting with the wisdom of nature: hearing the birds sing, blowing gently in the wind. With your hands in the clay, head in the clear air, and heart in nature, nurturing the garden fosters feelings of peacefulness and connectedness that help feed not just the body but the soul.

Motivation from within

You were born to exercise. Primitive man was a hunter and gatherer, running many miles on a daily basis, gathering berries while escaping the clutches of lions and big brown bears! Now, your day is more likely to be spent sitting at a desk, behind the wheel of a car or slouched in front of a computer or TV screen. Of course this doesn't describe everyone, but you get the picture.

Despite all the known benefits, many people choose to laze around, procrastinate and simply do not take enough exercise to stay healthy. And you know what? Many doctors are no exception here either. Despite all the medical evidence about the health benefits of exercise, some doctors either conveniently ignore this information or live in denial.

Maybe you're not motivated; maybe you believe you are too busy. There's no doubt the pace of modern life can squeeze time – your most precious commodity. Yet time is always made available for anything urgent that crops up, while things that are invaluable to your long-term health, such as regular exercise, can be omitted, forgotten or put on the long finger. Perhaps you are planning on taking more exercise at some time in the future when you are more organised and less busy?

Unfortunately, for many people the reality is that that day never comes. Look at the shocking rates of heart disease and the explosion of obesity-related conditions, such as diabetes, and you will quickly realise that procrastination won't get you anywhere. Those who don't make time for exercise eventually make time for illness.

The key is that to really enjoy the health benefits of exercise, it must be regular. Unlike occasional deposits in a bank account, you can't store up the benefits of exercise, so a mad burst of activity once a week just won't do the trick. It's never too late to reap the game-changing benefits of exercise, no matter how old you think you are or how unfit you may be right now. They say every journey of a thousand miles begins with a single step; take that first step today and make exercise part of a better, healthier you.

It can take sixty-six days to build a new habit; that's a long time and may explain why change can be so difficult. You are a creature of habit (we all are!) and will tend to stay on automatic pilot, thinking, feeling and doing what you have always been thinking, feeling and doing. Staying familiar with what's familiar! But if you have the courage to maintain a new habits that, over time, become so engrained that you do them automatically, subconsciously, just like brushing your teeth. Think of a new habit that you could adopt that would make you happier (and as a result healthier!). Eating more healthily, taking more exercise, or spending more time on those things that are important for you.

To achieve your potential you must break those habits that are holding you back and build those habits that support you in achieving the success you desire. The truth is, the results you have in your life right now are a reflection of your current habits. If you're interested in something but really not that committed, then you are only going to do it when it is convenient for you, when the sun is shining, when the wind is at your back. You need to be passionately committed not just pleasantly interested; when you are really committed to something there are no excuses, no places to hide. By dropping some of those self-defeating habits that may prevent you from achieving your true potential (clutter, distractions, too much television, time wasters, listening to needless negativity), you can channel more of your energy into expanding your happiness.

is more conducive to optimal psychological fitness, emotional happiness and great relationships. Not bad for a commitment of upwards of only half an hour a day.

Know your why! Remember exercise is a great form of self-investment, the greatest pill of all. People sometimes say they don't have the energy to exercise but if you persevere with your new exercise habit for two months or more, your energy levels will soar.

So make a regular exercise programme a priority for your happiness and well-being. The only rule about exercise is that there are no rules. To get the maximum health benefits from exercise, this magic health pill needs to be taken regularly. Exercise, ideally on a daily basis, but at least four to five times a week. After that you are free to choose whatever works best for you. Plan ahead. If necessary sleep in your gym clothes! (Or put them and your trainers right beside the bed.) Set your alarm an hour earlier so you have time to exercise in the morning. Use your journal to monitor your progress, recording what you've done, and how you felt before and after. Knowing how good you felt on those days you exercised even though you didn't feel like it beforehand can be a powerful motivator to keep going. Keeping a record of your exercise habits can give you more insight into how much (or how little) exercise you are really taking over a week and help you to include exercise as an important part of your schedule. By looking at your time in chunks of a week at a time, you can plan more effectively. Ask these questions in your journal. What are your exercise goals (short, medium and long term)? Write them down! Make yourself accountable. What's the one thing you can do today to get you started? What physical activities do you like most? Can you make them part of your schedule? What programmes best fit your schedule? How can you adjust your schedule to benefit from the game-changing benefits of exercise? Do you prefer to exercise alone or as part of a group? Every journey begins with that first step. Start small, and build up gradually. Remember, small daily improvements over time can transform your fitness, shrink your waistline and expand your happiness.

Remember the 5 Fs of exercise
- Fitness
- Flexibility
- Feeling great
- Fun
- For a happier YOU!

The Seventh Commitment:

Realistic Optimism – Oxygen for Opportunity

Mark Pollock is an extraordinary man. When he was five, a detached retina resulted in complete blindness in his right eye. Temporary episodes of total blindness occurred throughout his childhood. As a young athlete he was a champion rower, competing for Trinity College Dublin, and winning medals at the Commonwealth Games for Northern Ireland. At the age of twenty-two, the retina detached in his good left eye. He described his feelings of futility, of being unable to appreciate night from day, of being weighed down by the barriers of now permanent blindness.

However, he displayed remarkable resilience to bounce back and become an elite ultra-endurance athlete in events that took him across the world, even to polar ice caps! He described how he spent up to sixteen hours a day dragging sledges on skis in the company of Norwegian Special Forces, ex-Royal Marines and double Olympic gold medallists, to become the first blind man ever to reach the South Pole.

Even more adversity awaited him when he accidentally fell from a second storey window. He suffered horrific injuries including a fractured skull and bleeding on the brain resulting in near death. Having spent months in hospital he left in a wheelchair, permanently paralysed below the waist.

And now he wants to get out of his wheelchair, to be a pioneer in the world of spinal injury, to dream of a world empty of wheelchairs.

In an extraordinary display of courage he has made a documentary, Unbreakable, about his experiences to date. In this film, he highlights the difficult complications of paralysis: not alone the absence of movement and feeling but lack of bladder or bowel function, sexual problems, infections, pain, contractures and temperature control.

He speaks about the fact that without acceptance of the reality of how things are, there is no start line. But without hope, there is no finish line. Creating a space between these two points, of acceptance and hope, opens up the possibility of dreaming about the way that things can be and expecting problems while exploring new possibilities.

Mark's journey into the space of possibility has seen him become a real pioneer as the first person in the world to own a pair of bionic robotic legs. As a global speaker and advocate for spinal injury, the mission of his trust (MarkPollockTrust. Org) is to find people around the world to foster further collaboration so as to fast-track a cure for paralysis.

I was privileged to meet Mark recently when he spoke in Waterford, and was genuinely moved and inspired by his courage and determination to make a difference. When I think of realistic optimism, I can think of no finer example of a person who, while accepting reality, by his ongoing efforts is able to hope for the possibility of a brighter future.

The word resilient comes from the Latin word 'resilio', meaning to bounce back from adversity. It also implies healthy coping and, of course, realistic optimism. This ability to keep going in the face of setbacks and bounce back with purpose is a key characteristic of realistic optimism. When you have experienced being knocked down in life, getting up again makes you feel truly alive. You have decided that, no matter what, you are going to do your best to make it happen. Resilient people have more grit and determination to keep going; they acknowledge risk but are more likely to be future-orientated, hopeful and positive in outlook. This ability to cultivate realistic optimism and look on the bright side of things is at the very core of resilience.

Imagine five years from now and everything you work so hard towards turns out just the way you plan it. Use your journal to write about and describe this 'best possible future self': how everything will look five years from now, when you achieve some of your goals and everything works out for the best. Because of your self-belief, and through your own efforts – being creative, resourceful and open to new possibilities – you are reaching your full potential. In this respect, realistic optimism – knowing that it is possible – can become the foundation of a self-fulfilling prophecy. Having that inner strength to know that no matter what, you are going to make it happen.

Wouldn't that be exciting for you? What do you expect your life will look like in this imagined future? How will it feel? Describing in detail your best possible future can be a powerful way to reframe your beliefs and build your sense of realistic optimism. Also describe the character strengths that you will use to make this best possible future self a reality for you. Writing in this manner can give you a roadmap for your future: a concrete plan to move you forward.

Mark Twain wrote eloquently that 'It isn't the things we did that we most regret; it's the things we didn't do.' Have the courage to follow your dreams. Develop the inner confidence to live a life true to yourself, not simply reacting to the expectations of others.

Visualise this best possible future in detail. Write about and describe this vision in detail in your journal. Visualising in detail can have a significant boost on positivity and happiness. How visualisation works remains unclear; perhaps it may give you unique insights into the connection between your everyday experiences and your future dreams. Perhaps it's laying the foundations of a roadmap to your future, by activating the same brain areas you use to carry out those same visualised actions. Visualisation can be especially good for long-term goals like writing a book (and as I'm working at my computer writing this book, I'm visualising you reading it, meaning I have finally finished what I started and got it published!).

Oxygen for Opportunity

I call optimism the oxygen for opportunity in life. Of course, when I mention the word optimism, I am not referring to blind irrational optimism, so often a distorted, delusional and ultimately self-destructive Pollyanna vision of the future. Instead, focus on realistic optimism: the belief that things can get better because you are going to do something about it.

And realistic optimism is a *choice*, not just wishful thinking. Each day you can choose to wake up grumpy or with a cheerful, positive outlook.

The late Dale Carnegie wrote in his book, *How to Stop Worrying and Start Living*, that two men looked out from prison bars: one saw the mud, the other saw stars. This tendency to see the world as you are, rather than as it is, means your ability to develop your sense of realistic optimism can be learned and cultivated. By looking at the opportunity in every challenging situation, you can learn to see the glass as half-full rather than half-empty. Realistic optimism is this commitment to turn your 'can I or can't I, will I or wont I?' into 'when will I and how?' In so doing, by the power of your own efforts, you increase the likelihood of these events becoming reality. So don't throw the baby out with the bathwater; learn to turn your stumbling blocks into stepping stones of opportunity by cultivating the happiness-building habit of realistic optimism.

Being optimistic is good for your health, plain and simple. People who are more optimistic tend to be physically healthier with a stronger immune system. Being optimistic can reduce your risk of heart disease, whereas pessimism can be very bad for your heart, probably as a result of all those poison dwarfs!

In Japan the concept of *Ikigai* (pronounced eek-y-guy) means a reason to get up in the morning and enjoy life. Rooted in the conviction that one's life is worth living, it implies meaning as well as optimism. Research from Japan shows that lack of *Ikigai* is associated with increased risk of death due to heart disease. In the culture of Okinawa, *Ikigai* is thought to be one of the reasons why people living there have such long lives.

Realistic optimism strengthens your psychological fitness as you become more aware of your thinking patterns and beliefs. It can help protect you from accurately seeing the pain and challenges that the future may hold, which can be a good thing at times. Rather than take negative thoughts at face value, you can learn to dispute them and come up with alternative more positive solutions. Learning to reframe challenging situations in a more positive way allows you to dissipate negative stress, deal better with the poison dwarfs and help tip the scales of positivity back in your direction.

Realistic optimism energises the happy dwarf called Hope; as a result you feel happier, more confident and willing to believe 'it is possible'.

Importance of vision

When people speak about range of vision, traditionally what is meant is your ability to see. I like to distinguish between two different terms: eyesight and mind sight. Certainly your eyes allow you to see what's in front of you, but your mind allows you to see what's before you. And there are two distinct types of mind sight: closed and open. Because you tend to see the world not as it is but as you are, the type of mind sight you choose can have a major impact on how you lead your life. How you pay attention to your inner self-talk predicts much more about your future potential than you may think.

This ability of your own worldview to significantly impact on your life has been brilliantly described by Carol S. Dweck in her groundbreaking book *Mindset: How You Can Fulfil Your Potential*. If you have a closed mind sight, you believe that your talents are set in stone; that you have a certain amount of intelligence, and ability. This becomes not only a self-measure of your potential but also a limitation of that potential. With the closed mind sight you either have it or you don't. There is no point in trying, life has dealt you a hand and that's it. You tend to look down on effort – surely you can't be that good if you have to work that hard. If you have success with the closed mind sight, you may develop 'impostor syndrome' – believing you are going to be found out! And dealing with failure can be even more problematic: what to do when your special talent isn't enough to succeed? Every situation tends to become win/lose; will I succeed or fail; will I be accepted or rejected? In the closed mind sight, everything is about the outcome, the destination rather than the journey (all-or-nothing thinking). So you tend to shy aware from challenges and stay in the comfort zone to try to avoid the possibility of failure. If at first you don't succeed you tend to give up, allowing the poison dwarfs called Fear and Anxicty to rule the roost.

With an open mind sight, you believe your natural gifts and

talents are simply the beginning: a starting point from which you can improve through the application of dedicated effort. The focus here is on improvement and on personal growth: on progress, not perfection. Here, it's all about the journey of improvement, not the destination. You see challenges as learning opportunities; your mind is open to new possibilities and you believe and understand that your true potential is not only unknown but unknowable.

For several thousand years, philosophers and scientists from ancient China, Egypt and Rome devoted their lives to the *Magnum Opus* – the search for the philosopher's stone. Legend had it that the philosopher's stone was the key element in alchemy: turning common metals like lead into silver or gold and in so doing, a panacea, creating an elixir of life to cure all forms of illness. I believe the real search for the philosopher's stone is the one which lies within you: with an open mind sight, the human brain can adapt rapidly to your circumstances and be masterful at turning lead into gold.

To develop your own philosopher's stone, use your journal to reflect on your experiences and reframe challenging situations to find the silver lining. Learn to learn in a new and different way: consider the opportunities you have today for learning and for growth. Become more resilient; reward your efforts and commitment to improvement. Use your previous experiences as an opportunity to learn, and to grow. Ask yourself: 'What can I learn from that experience?' 'Can I use that experience as a basis for future growth?' 'How can I improve?' Remember that actions speak louder than words; your self-belief will be exposed to others through what you do, and how you do it, much more than by what you say.

Anticipate the challenges you will meet along the way. Don't allow so-called failure or criticism to define you; create emotional strategies to deal with it. Have an action plan for failure and for success and recognise the golden opportunity to learn from so-called failure. Use this feedback to open up the boundless possibilities that your life contains to flourish in the face of change, challenge and opportunity. When you succeed, ask yourself, 'What do I have to do to maintain and continue the growth?' Be persistent. Keep a sense of perspective. Make your own development and growth a written goal. Write it down in your journal!

Stepping Stones to Realistic Optimism

The Chinese writer Lutang wrote: 'Prepare for the worst but expect the best.' Doing this sets you free but leaves you with the possibility of everything to gain. Just like happiness, some people are naturally more optimistic than others. But your degree of optimism is not set in stone. Realistic optimism is a skill that can be learned, developed and improved upon.

Realistic optimists tend to see life's challenges as being temporary, controllable and specific to one situation. They are naturally able to downplay negative thoughts and feelings and have a better coping style. They don't ignore problems – far from it, they face them head on and pay more attention to the silver lining of every dark cloud. Realistic optimists understand that setbacks are an inevitable part of life but they are more effective at navigating those setbacks and avoiding the pitfalls. They neither take things personally nor turn their molehills into mountains. Instead they plan, persist and persevere, coming up with new solutions and becoming more resilient. Realistic optimism is about seeing setbacks and so-called failures as opportunities to grow and learn something useful and to ultimately become stronger.

Use your journal to write down negative thinking patterns that you experience and reframe them with more optimistic thoughts. Watch out for perfectionist, all-or-nothing-type thinking patterns, 'excusitis', etc. Realistic optimism allows you to weed out negative non-productive thoughts and to replace them with more constructive thoughts; it supports your letting go, moving on to healthy coping and psychological growth. Use your journal to expand the range of positive outcomes to any given situation. If you define the possible outcomes too narrowly and those outcomes fail to materialise, you are going to feel disappointed. Look at your own past mistakes, own them, learn from and grow beyond them. By including the possibility of learning something useful about yourself and others, of meeting people and having experiences you otherwise would not have had, it is much easier to have perspective, to stay positive and optimistic.

Write positive affirmations and optimistic statements in your journal; read and reread them regularly. For example: 'I can control my attitude'; 'Every journey begins with a single step'; 'Small daily improvements over time can lead to amazing results.'

Cultivating realistic optimism can galvanise your mood and morale, motivating you to invest more time and effort in working towards your important goals. Remember practice makes improvement; commit to the journey, innovate or stagnate! Don't strive for perfection, it doesn't exist! By having at least several goals on the go at any one time, you can avail of the happiness spillover effect – which means that if you make progress in one area of your life, this tends to spill over into other areas. Choose to focus on what you can do; ask yourself what is the one thing I can do right now to make a difference?

There is a saying that when one door closes in life, another door opens. So true! Understand that every stumbling block of adversity in life can be a stepping stone to even greater opportunity if you protect your thinking and focus on the opportunity. Remember that the darkest hour comes before the dawn. Ultimately the most important thing about any setback is how you allow that setback to define you and what you do to bounce back. Understand the role you have played in your current circumstances, and that the key to making a change comes from your own efforts. Be ambitious, conscientious and self-disciplined; learn the value of effort and endurance. Appreciate that the only real constant in life is change; and that change leads to new possibilities and fresh opportunities.

Epictetus, the philosopher, wrote that 'some things are up to us, and some things are not.' Be really clear about what you can change and what you can't.

Imagine a beautiful butterfly, struggling to squeeze its way out of a tiny crack in its cocoon. It is really striving and making a great effort to get its head through the small hole but its body seems too large; it is getting nowhere fast. After a long struggle, it appears to give up, remaining absolutely still, exhausted. Suppose you decide to help this butterfly; with a pair of scissors you slice open the cocoon allowing it to escape. But instead of opening its wings and flying, its dysmorphic-looking features with shrunken body and shrivelled wings crawl around as you watch expectantly, waiting for it to fly.

But it never gets to fly because it didn't get to struggle; the effort required to get out of the cocoon was nature's way of squeezing fluid from the body into the wings, so necessary to strengthen them for flight. This butterfly died without ever soaring high or achieving his potential. In life, the struggle and extra effort can be your greatest opportunity to express your best, to grow and become the best possible version of YOU.

The Eighth Commitment:

Simplicity – The Ultimate Sophistication

As Socrates wrote, beware the barrenness of a busy life. Paul – let's call him that – was at breaking point when I saw him in my practice. Several years of overwork, the physical and mental strain of trying to be all things to everyone, had eventually taken their toll. On top of that, negative equity, burgeoning debts and bank threats had left him emotionally (if not financially) bankrupt. With mild depressive symptoms, relationship issues and so much negative stress, his life was definitely on a downward spiral.

Paul needed treatment to escape those dark hours: not just medication, but talking therapy and a fundamental realignment of his life to his values. The relentless pursuit of more had left him empty, exhausted and emotionally flat with constant feelings of failure and futility.

By being encouraged to keep a journal, Paul became more self-aware of how negative thoughts were holding him back and better able to reframe situations in a more positive light. He set some goals for his physical health and his own development as a person. To his credit he had the courage and commitment to make long-lasting and sustainable changes in his life. He learned how to express gratitude regularly by writing about those things he felt genuinely grateful for. He learned about the power of building great exercise habits and using his journal to monitor them. He began to reduce his exposure to negative noise in the media and in his relationships. He learned how to use his experiences as the basis for improvements in his psychological fitness and his relationships. Small improvements, step by step, with the focus at all times on progress, not perfection.

Two years later, Paul has steadily and mindfully embraced a life of simplicity. Today he is unrecognisable from his former self. He had the courage to take back control of his life. The result – a complete personal transformation. Not only is he physically much leaner and fitter, he feels so much better in himself, his relationships have improved and his life is on an upward spiral. He is healthier, off medication, more engaged with his children, more in touch with his emotions, and feels much happier.

Living more in the moment

The Chinese philosopher Zhuangzi once wrote that happiness is the absence of the striving for happiness; that ultimate happiness is achieved when you learn to let go and simply engage in activities for their own sake without any hidden agendas. This allows you to be more spontaneous and childlike; at the highest level you can transcend your ego and merge with the Dao, or 'the way', the underlying unity that embraces all things.

Simplicity is being able to live in the here and now, to be present-orientated. Doing your best to enjoy each moment of every day is a key ingredient in your happiness and well-being. The past is nothing more than memories and the future nothing more than thoughts and images in the present.

Staying in the moment is not easy. So often, people are either stuck in the past or fretting about the future and as a result, they miss out on the present – so much time, given away for free! So slow down and *be* more. The funny thing is the present moment (right now as you are reading this) is *all* you have so appreciate everything you have in your life right now. Allow yourself to be present where you are at this moment; derive pleasure, engagement and meaning today. Today is the tomorrow you may have worried about yesterday. By not paying attention to the present moment, you are denying yourself the experience of what is really happening right now for what may or may not happen at some point in the future. Live more in the moment; move away from the regrets of the past or anxiety about the future, towards a happier, more meaningful present. Try it and live the difference!

Keeping a journal can make you more aware of the connection you have with your environment, and the emotional, visual and situational cues that you may be reacting to in your life. Write down how they make you feel and consider how you could make some changes or improvements to experience more of this emotional enhancement.

Connecting with your environment in this way can become a continuous conversation, as you better appreciate the beautiful simplicity of spending more time in nature. Immersing yourself in nature can fully occupy your attention and awareness, giving you a real positivity boost in terms of your mood. Your thinking becomes more creative and expansive, giving you more things to feel good about.

Every breath you take, sound you hear, sight you see, flavour you taste, fragrance you smell, and sensation you experience registers in your consciousness. Together, they can become a physical reminder of the power of the environment you live and work in to impact on your happiness and well-being. So have a number of favourite spots that are regular and easy to access destinations for you; places you can get to quickly, whether blue ocean, blue sky or a simple touch of greenery.

While realistic optimism is finding the good within the

bad, savouring is finding the good within the good, turning something positive into even more gold-plated positivity. Savouring is when you consciously take in your surroundings and experience your emotions with a powerful sense of appreciation for what is happening in that moment. You give deliberate attention to the experience of pleasure. Whereas flow involves complete immersion in the zone, savouring requires you to slightly step outside of the experience, just enough to really enjoy it. Savouring is that balance between experiencing fully the richness of the moment with being able to look forward (or back) with an eager sense of anticipation (or reflection). Remember how good something felt. How did something taste, feel or smell? What could you touch and see?

Savouring is *not* analysis; asking why something was so good or why it can't always be like this is a sure-fire way to reduce positive feelings, causing paralysis by analysis!

Savouring has significant benefits for your emotional well-being; you become happier, less anxious and more resilient in the face of obstacles. Savouring includes the capacity to plan ahead: experience happiness by simply looking forward to something with joy and with a sense of anticipation and expectation. Imagine the time spent thinking about your upcoming break, the exhilaration of anticipating your family holiday. Being able to savour an approaching event means you are much more likely to be resilient and happy in the belief that good things are coming your way. As a result of this, you will act in ways that will help ensure the future you are envisioning.

Savouring includes the ability to look back and reminisce about what you have already done, taking great joy and pleasure from those memories. This type of savouring is often called reminiscing. It not only increases happiness but can allow you to create much more meaning from your life. This can be so much better when you share this memory with a friend, and then listen to their experience.

Imagine you have tickets for your favourite band who are playing next weekend; these tickets are like gold dust and you are so excited! Beforehand you might say, this concert is going to be great. During the event you might say to yourself, I'm taking it all in. After the event you might replay and relive all the positive aspects of the night with family or friends. In this way you can multiply the feel-good factor threefold by extracting more positivity before, during and after an uplifting experience. Three times the enjoyment for the price of one!

There are simply so many ways to improve your ability to savour. Try savouring the aroma of your freshly brewed coffee, or the sensuality of a refreshing shower or relaxing bath. Reminisce with a family member or friend, keep photo albums or vision boards of happy times together. Build memories; keep pictures, scrap books or albums of happy times everywhere. Really enjoy some event you would normally rush through, for example cooking a delicious meal. Learn to meditate; shut out the noise and become more fully absorbed in the moment, creating moments of stillness and solitude. Become more aware of your senses as you experience, for example, the delights of a delicious meal. Celebrate and reminisce with loved ones or friends; regular storytelling helps savouring to flourish in families. Shared experiences with others can be one of the best ways to feel more positive, and create an upward spiral of well-being.

Be good to yourself! Celebrate and reward yourself for a job well done; reflect how hard you have worked and how long you have waited to achieve a certain goal, no matter how small. Build new experiences in your life; they'll be good for the brain and help to prevent hedonic adaptation. Use your journal to consider a weekly savouring day as an opportunity to stop and take stock of your life; small things can be the big things.

Mindfulness

Being more mindful is a great way to embrace simplicity, allowing you to be more present, to luxuriate in the present moment and to experience more of its vibrancy and richness. Mindfulness is paying attention on purpose, being more aware of what you are doing while you are actually doing it. This cultivation of conscious awareness allows you to be more open, to appreciate an acceptance – without judgement or analysis – of whatever you are experiencing in the present moment. Mindfulness builds self-awareness: acknowledging, accepting, even appreciating disruptions and allowing them to pass.

Easy ways to practise mindfulness: when taking a shower, experience the water flowing over you and be fully present. Try mindful eating: use all your senses to experience each mouthful of food, slowly and deliberately.

Benefits of being more mindful include greater focus and clarity about the present moment: deriving more enjoyment from a positive experience by mindfully slowing down to take it all in. Mindfulness supports building more healthy habits and breaking old habits; it encourages greater connectedness with others and reduces stress. Overall a more mindful approach to life can expand your happiness. Try it and see for yourself.

Making Time to Declutter

Through my opportunity to work with the principles of health design leadership, I began to appreciate how the space you work and live in influences your health, happiness and well-being. I began to understand the representational value of clutter: not the clutter per se, but what it represented. Understanding that a cluttered desk does not (I repeat does not) equate with a clearly flowing, organised mind. This appreciation of the connectedness of all things was a real 'aha' moment for me, and so clutter became a representation of how I valued myself and the people I was sharing the space with. On another level, clutter may be seen as a sign of procrastination; for many people, the mere thought of having to deal with it is too overwhelming to overcome their inertia.

In the feng shui process, decluttering is the first step in the process that allows energy to flow freely. Do you need to declutter your physical space? The physical space in which you work and live can impact on your thinking and exploring this through your journal can help you to declutter and free up some vital energy. Creating the space to be creative can help you to become much more focused, purposeful and intentional with your thoughts and with the environment that allows those thoughts to develop.

Your life can become more peaceful: creating more time and energy, experiencing more of a sense of freedom. Less time spent looking for things, and less emotional attachment to stuff. This process can take several months and can be so liberating and empowering; try it and experience the benefits for your happiness and well-being. By learning to let go of what no longer fits in your home, office or in yourself, you will feel happier, as a clearer space is supportive, revitalising and comforting.

Regarding some decluttering tips: start small, the smallest of actions is better than the noblest of intentions. Develop the habit of doing things now rather than putting them off for later. What you do everyday matters so much more than what you do once in a while! Breaking a task into bite-sized chunks can make it so much more enjoyable; think of the smallest action you can take and then just do it. Focus on one corner of your desk or one drawer at a time; have a 'to do' list. Do a virtual move; ask yourself if you were moving home, would you bring or leave this? Keep what's essential: donate, dump, recycle the rest. Involve others: teach your children to be responsible for their own spaces. Address underlying emotional issues, if any (for example poison dwarfs like Fear; of loss or of insecurity). Get out of your own way; observe your resistance to change! Let go of clutter to make more room for you; enjoy the journey, find more simplicity and have fun!

From technological overload, and task-laden busyness agendas, to testing relationships, the world you live in now is full of complexity. One of the downsides of the information age is the endless availability of distractions with e-mail, social media and smart phones creating a never-ending demand for your attention. How often do you get an e-mail reminding you to appreciate your partner or invest more time with your family? Consider putting yourself on a technology diet. Just as you can choose not to stock your cupboards with junk food, so you can limit your exposure to the web and enjoy it in the limited window that you give yourself. Have you ever considered a digital detox – a technology-free time in your day, week, and life? Try it and see how it feels!

Simplicity allows you to peel back the layers of stuff (physical and emotional), to reveal more of your true nature and authentic self. Leonardo Da Vinci wrote: 'Simplicity is the ultimate sophistication.' Simplicity will bring heightened awareness of and clarity about what's most important, freeing you up to experience more of the moments that become lifelong memories. Your personal spaces can become a safe haven where you can relax in comfort and schedule some 'me' time, no longer hidden behind the clutter and concerns of everyday life. As you become more present minded, you will experience more joy from those simple things in life: birds singing, a fabulous sunset, time with friends and family. Consider the simplicity of a walk on the beach, feeling the wind at your back.

By choosing to simplify your life, control your distractions, and reduce your level of exposure to negative noise, you can focus on the positive thoughts that produce more positive results in your life. By choosing to think differently and focus on what's right, you can appreciate more positive things and create an upward spiral of positivity. Less stuff can be more, so much more! Remember small incremental steps over time can transform your life with confidence and boldness to one of true simplicity and abundant happiness.

My '6 Ss' which can support a sense of simplicity include silence, stillness, solitude, security, serenity and sophistication. Solitude and spending some time alone can foster freedom, creativity and an enhanced capacity for intimacy when you return.

Ask yourself in your journal: do you put off living in the present? How can you embrace more simplicity? When are you going to start this?

The Ninth Commitment:

Spirituality - The Purpose of Life is a Life of Purpose

Back in the middle ages, when the Earth was believed to be at the very centre of the universe, Nicolaus Copernicus' radical paradigm-shifting suggestion that the Earth rotates on its axis around the sun was not met initially with widespread approval. Far from it! Despite his theory being first published initially in 1543, it was up to two hundred years later before his ideas were widely accepted.

And fast forward to today with our ever expanding sense of space and the universe. There are currently estimated to be a hundred billion galaxies, each of which contain around a hundred billion stars! What would they have thought back then of the idea of space travel? Socrates, the Greek philosopher, said nearly three thousand years ago that humanity must rise above the earth, to the top of the atmosphere and beyond, to understand the world in which we live. Samadhi is the Sanskrit term for an experience of seeing things in their separateness, but also to transcend the sense of separateness and experience a sense of unity, accompanied by ecstasy.

Edgar Mitchell became the sixth man ever to walk on the moon during the Apollo 14 mission in 1971. He described how, on the way back home to Earth, he became aware of an inexplicable euphoria and whole body experience which had a transformative impact on him. He began to see things in a larger perspective than ever before with a new sense of appreciation of the connectedness between Earth, the heavens and the entire galaxy: a realisation that we are all part of the same stuff, connected to the stars. The result: Edgar Mitchell developed a new awareness of all systems in the universe being part of a synergistic whole; this in turn led him to a renewed sense of responsibility for humanity and the environment.

This sense of awe, accompanied by feelings of timelessness and bliss, is shared by many astronauts. Earth seen from the vantage point of space creates a cosmic connection, the sense of one species with one destiny sharing one ecosystem, protected by a paper-thin atmosphere, beautiful yet fragile. Thousands of years ago Heraclitus, the philosopher, was one of the first to consider this connectedness of all things. He wrote about the Logos, a cosmic intelligence that guides and unifies the universe. The Logos implies that everything is part of the bigger picture, that everything is beautiful. Looking down on the world through the eyes of the 'Big Picture' can instil more of a sense of wonder and awe, putting the worries and troubles of life into perspective.

A PRESCRIPTION FOR HAPPINESS

The White Light of Spirituality

In many ways this sense of connectedness and of being part of something much greater than yourself is at the very heart of spirituality. The Oxford English Dictionary defines spirituality as 'the real sense of significance of something.' It is a search for the sacred, for meaning, comfort and inner peace in your life; a relationship with a higher being or force, such as nature or God. Many people find spirituality through religion; some find it through art, music, or connecting with nature; others in the daily practice of their life values. Spirituality is about having the courage to understand the journey of your life, to live out your dreams and fulfil your potential. You are hardwired to be spiritual, imaginative and inquisitive. Improving your spiritual well-being may help you feel better physically, psychologically and emotionally. If you find your activities to be significant and meaningful, then you are far more likely to experience spirituality and happiness.

The body, mind and spirit all appear linked in an interdependent manner. By connecting to something larger than yourself, you can cultivate a sense of gratitude and more positive feelings such as awe amazement, and happy dwarfs and especially Inspiration.

Spirituality can be a highly effective coping strategy to deal with all the poison dwarfs that illness can bring, providing peace of mind, inner security and serenity. The emotional comfort and strength gained from spirituality can enhance your self-esteem, boost confidence, and contribute to healing. Spirituality can help you fight feelings of helplessness and bring on the happy dwarf called Hope: knowing that what you do and who you are ultimately matters.

Spirituality includes self-reflection and insight into questions about your authenticity. As well as helping you discover your true self, self-understanding involves being more considerate and tolerant of the values and beliefs of others which may well differ from your own. From a psychological fitness viewpoint spirituality can give you more of a sense of self-acceptance; accepting yourself for who you really are (including your imperfections and shortcomings) and taking one hundred per cent responsibility for your own life.

For years I have admired the work of the artist Salvador Dali: so synonymous with creativity, innovation and freedom of personal identity. He described his ideal building as being a living thing with walls that move in and out like lungs. Wow! What out-of-the-box thinking! I love his use of contrasts, how he combines the classical with the fantastical, from Apollo, the Greek god of the sun (the clarity of light and the sense of order it brings to the world) to Dionysus, god of the grape harvest (disorderly, ecstatic, the blur and sensuality of wine).

Dali challenges the viewer to remember that the world changes according to the way you look at it: that you do see things as you are! One of his paintings in particular captured my imagination. Entitled *Nature Morte Vivante (Still Life-Fast Moving) 1956*, familiar still-life objects circle each other in suspended animation, with water being poured 'in reverse' against gravity from a drinking glass into a glass bottle below it.

That idea of the water flowing from the glass to the jug stayed with me, and got me thinking about the rainbow, with its seven colours (Red, Orange, Yellow, Green, Blue, Indigo, Violet); just like the Seven Happy Dwarfs (Joy, Hope, Interest, Inspiration, Enthusiasm, Fun and the giant of unconditional Love). Now some people spend their lives chasing the rainbow, and the elusive crock of gold that lies at the end, just like chasing happiness!

But there is no need to do that because the potential for expanding your happiness lies within you right now; you can choose to cultivate the Seven Happy Dwarfs (the rainbow of happiness and well-being).

A PRESCRIPTION FOR HAPPINESS

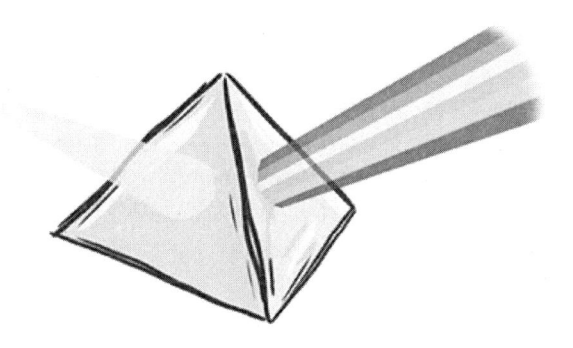

Have you seen white light being diffracted through a glass prism, producing the seven colours of the rainbow? Not too much imagination required here as any self-respecting science buff will tell you. But now try this in reverse (just as Dali did in the painting with the glass and jug of water): suppose those seven colours went in reverse back through the prism, producing white light. For me this is the very essence of spirituality: cultivating the Seven Happy Dwarfs and mixing them through the prism. No ordinary prism but one filled with heartfelt compassion, healthy humility, authenticity, gratitude, empathy and simplicity: a journey of inner transformation, leading to the white light of spirituality.

Freud, the psychoanalyst, described religion as 'the universal compulsive neurosis of mankind', emphasising the negative impact of religion in terms of it producing feelings of guilt, repression and intolerance.

However, in recent years, new understandings have emerged that religious belief can provide significant health benefits irrespective of whether you are Buddhist, Christian, Hindu or Muslim. The sense of forgiveness and compassion for others that religious belief cultivates can build coping skills and resilience, and strengthen psychological fitness. Through the sense of community, relationships can be strengthened by the significant social support that involvement in religious organisations provides. Happiness and emotional well-being can be boosted by the higher levels of realistic optimism and the encouragement of happy dwarfs such as Hope, Love and Joy. Religion tends, for the most part, to encourage moderation and a low-stress healthier lifestyle; as a result, people with religious belief tend to be happier, better connected to their families and more satisfied with life overall.

Meditation

'Learn to be silent.
Let your
quiet mind
listen and absorb.'
PYTHAGORAS (580 BC TO 500 BC)

Meditation is a wonderful way to declutter and detox your mind from distractions, clearing out all the chatter, noise and turbulence, to quieten the mind and simply 'be.' You focus your energy on 'being' (being still, open, trusting and patient), experiencing mental quietness, stillness or pure consciousness. By becoming more aware of the present moment of each thought, observing it impartially, accepting it for what it is (whether good or bad) and letting it pass, you appreciate better that everything works out in its own good time.

Meditation is about finding the path back to your true nature. By cultivating your attention, you become more attuned to your thoughts, emotions and interactions with others. As a very personal experience, meditation challenges you to temporarily withdraw from the urgency of the world around you, from the noise of all those distractions (internet, television, radio), from conversation, speaking, even from thinking. It allows you to practise non-judgement, to detach yourself emotionally from your surroundings, your relationships and from life itself.

A PRESCRIPTION FOR HAPPINESS

St Francis De Sales (1567–1622) wrote that 'half an hour's meditation each day is essential, except when you are busy, when a full hour is needed.' Be generous and give yourself the gift of daily meditation; let your life develop in a new direction. Meditation is a wonderful way to experience pure silence and pure awareness, free from attachment or from trying to rush or force things. Meditation gives you access to those innermost parts of your being that are fearless, creative and alive. As you develop mastery over your attention, you will become aware of every little thing as though seeing it for the very first time. Imagine the ripple effect in a very still pond after you throw in a pebble; this is how your enhanced level of awareness can detect even the slightest ripple from the stillness. Without quietening your mind through meditation, a tidal wave could crash through the pond in your mind and you might not blink an eye or notice a thing.

Meditation appears to be one of the true silver bullets for improved health, strengthening the immune system, lowering blood pressure, reducing perception of chronic pain and enhancing well-being. Regular meditation supports better relationships by deepening your sense of connection with others, serving as a bridge between your material and spiritual aspects of being. Meditation can change your relationship with time, expanding and transcending your perceptions. By improving mental clarity, self-confidence and concentration, meditation strengthens psychological fitness, builds resilience and enhances your ability to deal with life's challenges. As you expand your horizons and enhance the search for fulfilment and meaning, you become calmer and better able to relax and recharge. Meditation can support your self-development as the path of knowledge becomes the path of wisdom, personal empowerment and transformation.

Fascinating groundbreaking research conducted by

A PRESCRIPTION FOR HAPPINESS

Dr Richard Davidson at the University of Wisconsin has identified a specific area of the brain associated with positive emotion and happiness (called the left prefrontal cortex). Having first measured the average level of activity in this happiness area of the brain among ordinary Americans, he repeated the same tests on monks from Tibet. Their higher levels of happiness related brain activity scores were off the charts! Subsequent research found that monks who meditate about compassion develop documented changes on functional MRI scans of their brains; specifically those parts of their brains that deal with positive emotion (the left prefrontal cortex) get bigger. In other words meditation can change the structure of your brain, making it more receptive to positivity; what you choose to think about really does matter in terms of expanding your happiness! Davidson describes how your brain patterns impact the way you think, feel and live in his book *The Emotional Life of Your Brain.*

To start to meditate choose a space that is quiet, comfortable and free of distractions. Get your posture right; sit alone on the floor or a chair with your legs crossed and spine straight while relaxing your back, neck and shoulders. Set an alarm to go off after a few minutes so that you can meditate free from the worries of time. Gradually build the length of time you meditate from five up to twenty minutes a day; the key is to do it regularly and build the habit. Close your eyes or gaze at an object in front of you like a lighted candle. Focus on your breathing as you breathe in and out.

Clear all distractions from your mind as you simply concentrate all your attention on your breathing; in and out, in and out, over and over again. Breathe in deeply and deliberately through your nose, with each breath filling up the space of your stomach, then breathe out slowly. Your breathing is an important link between your body and your mind; focus your breath on any part of your body that feels tense. What does your in-breath feel like? Be aware of the sensation of the breath as it enters your nostrils and gradually fills your lungs. What does each out-breath feel like? Be aware of each breath with a sense of detachment; each breath represents you here, right now in this moment. Try to focus on your breath to the exclusion of everything else. It takes a lot of practice and effort to keep your mind still, free from all those thoughts that want to rush in – known as the monkey mind! It's hard to free yourself from them and inevitably your mind will wander. That's OK; the key is to accept this, and start again. Make space for failure; commit to the journey, never stop starting! With practice and time, this small simple commitment to expand your happiness can become a game changer for your well-being as you become calmer, more content, and compassionate. There are many informal types of meditation you can engage in regularly. You can spend time silently communing with nature, watching the sun rise, listening to the sound of birds chirping or water flowing in a stream, practising yoga, taking aerobic exercise, or listening to inspirational music.

'Don't chase after the past, don't seek the future; the past is gone, the future hasn't come. But see clearly on the spot, that object which is now, while finding and living in a still, unmoving state of mind.'

BUDDHA.

All You Need Is Love

By writing in your journal and becoming more self-aware, you can identify those things in your life that give you a sense of comfort, meaning and inner strength. Then schedule some time regularly to do those things that you find help you spiritually. Everyone is different so what works for you may not work for others; do what you are comfortable with. This may simply mean quiet time for praying, meditating or attending religious services. However, things as diverse as spending time with nature, reading inspirational books, or helping others through volunteering can all boost your spiritual well-being.

Spirituality is also about learning to live in accordance with your values: guiding principles to support and motivate you as you move through life, like a compass giving your life its overall direction. Your values also represent the deepest desires of your heart: how you want to relate to and be in the world around you. Living by your values can give your life a rich and wonderful meaning: making more of an impact, living a life of contribution and real significance.

Maslow, a psychologist, became well known for devising a pyramid of human needs. Basic human requirements such as food, water and shelter were placed at the very bottom of the pyramid. At the very top or apex of the pyramid, self-actualisation; becoming all you can be, the highest known human experience. Later on he accepted there was something higher than being all you can be: self-transcendence, living for a higher purpose by committing your time, talents and energy to creating a lasting legacy, essential for a life of purpose and meaning.

Think about the change in attitude towards smoking, particularly passive smoking in the workplace, when a tipping point in public opinion was reached. Similarly I believe we are at the dawn of a new era of understanding, where compassion, considering the needs of others and a renewed and emergent sense of collective responsibility will signal a paradigm shift from 'what's in this for me?' to 'how can I be of service to others?'

Saint Francis of Assisi, the inspirational founder of the Franciscan order of monks in the early thirteenth century, referred to all living beings as his brothers and sisters. For me, his beautiful prayer is a powerful reminder of the potential possibility for spirituality in everyday life.

'Lord, make me an instrument of Your Peace.
Where there is hatred, let me sow love;
Where there is injury, pardon;
Where there is doubt, faith;
Where there is despair, hope;
Where there is darkness, light;
And where there is sadness, joy.
O Divine Master, grant that I may not so much seek
To be consoled as to console;
To be understood as to understand;
To be loved as to love;
For it is in giving that we receive;
It is in pardoning that we are pardoned;
And it is in dying that we are born to eternal light.'

The Tenth Commitment:

Courage – The Courage to Choose

Viktor Frankl was an Austrian psychiatrist who was incarcerated by the Nazis during World War II in Auschwitz – the most notorious of all of the Nazi death camps. He survived years of unspeakable horror there. In his awe-inspiring book Man's Search for Meaning, *he described how he and his friends, when stripped of all the bare necessities of life, could*

not in the final analysis be denied their human dignity.

In this fascinating account of his survival there, Frankl revealed that, in his experience, the people who survived longest in the death camps were not necessarily the fittest physically or the strongest but those who were most connected with a purpose and a mission in life. In his experience, if prisoners could connect with something they valued such as a loving relationship with their children, or some other unrealised goal, this deep connection gave them something to live for, something that made all the pain and all the suffering something they could better endure.

Despite all of their anguish, these prisoners still had the ability to choose how to respond in every given moment. It is your innate potential as a human being to choose how you react to any given set of circumstances. He also found that those not connected with a deeper value soon lost the will to live and developed a profound sense of hopelessness. One of Frankl's most deeply held values was helping others; throughout his time in the camps he listened compassionately to the tales of woe of other prisoners, giving words of kindness and inspiration. He consistently tried to support other prisoners to cope with their suffering and tended to the sick and the dying. Most importantly of all, he helped people to connect with their own deepest values so they could find a sense of meaning, which could, quite literally, give them the strength to survive. Frankl also deeply valued his loving relationship with his wife and he was determined to survive the camp so that one day he could see her again. He described how, while doing strenuous work in the snow, his body wracked with pain from brutal beatings and frostbitten feet, he would conjure up a mental image of his wife and focus on how much he loved her. This deep sense of connection was enough to keep him going through the deepest, darkest adversity, building his resilience and sense of realistic optimism. In the end, love conquers all. Despite the harrowing circumstances he found himself in, Frankl understood that he had the power to choose how to respond in any given moment. And by exercising that choice he described how he felt, in some ways, he had more freedom than his Nazi captors!

Be the change

There is an old Irish proverb which says to 'dance like no one's watching, sing like no one is listening, love like you've never been hurt, and live every day as if it were your last.'

By simply choosing to act happier you can raise your level of happiness. By thinking more positive thoughts and acting as you would like to feel, you can start to feel the way you act. Where's the catch? There is none.

If you hang around waiting for the right feeling to move you into action, then you may never get started. Simply choosing to act in a more confident, extroverted and energised manner can allow you to benefit from more positive feelings. And what's more, these are skills you can learn. Human nature dictates that people will tend to smile when they feel happy and frown when anxious. But the opposite may also be true; smiling can be a blueprint for feeling happier, your facial expressions can impact on your emotions. Perhaps the best way to act happier is by smiling more – not fake smiles but genuine heartfelt smiles. When you smile, you are telling your brain, 'I must be happy.' Facial expressions like smiling can play an important role in producing the positive feelings that accompany them.

This ability to express positive emotion by smiling is at the very heart of human relationships. Smiling is an outward sign of happiness and positive emotion, a free and easy way to boost your sense of well-being. Next time you are feeling the blues, chance a smile and your mood may well change for the better. Smiling can light up your face and make you look younger, a natural facelift. A smile has magnetism and charm, drawing others to you. You will be viewed by others as being more attractive, confident and self-assured. Emotions are contagious; smiling at someone encourages them to smile as well, brightening their mood and helping to make things better. A smile can brighten up even the darkest room and seeing others smile can make you feel happier. Be the change and smile your way to enhanced levels of health, happiness and more positivity. Smiling helps you to approach each day with gentleness and understanding. By triggering the release of serotonin (the happy hormone), smiling can boost your mood and is a natural antidote to stress, helping to dissolve worry, tension and fatigue from your appearance.

Life is a Journey

Pericles, the Greek orator from the Golden Age over 400 years BC, wrote that the secret to happiness is inner freedom and that the secret to inner freedom is courage. Having the courage to follow your dreams requires you to get out of your comfort zone and to face your fears, rather than simply reacting to the expectations of others. Courage is not the absence of fear but the willingness to walk through your fears in pursuit of something that's important for you.

Remember the importance of balance: actions *do* speak louder than words, so have the courage to show and tell those people that matter what they mean to you. It all comes down to love and relationships in the end. Have the courage to listen to your inner voice, express your feelings and face the truth of your life for what it really is. When your actions are motivated by your values, by the real you on the inside, your energy levels multiply and you are far more likely to create abundance in your life. By controlling your attention, building emotional vitality and cultivating relationships, you can achieve so much more of your true potential.

Life is about leadership, your ability to be more of a leader in your own life. And this leadership starts with your thinking! So watch your negative thoughts; they can cloud your thinking and make you feel more like a victim than a leader, turning your stepping stones into stumbling blocks. Thoughts are like leaves blowing in the wind, so when a negative thought blows into your mind, blow it out again by replacing it with a more positive thought. Become more creative and open to new possibilities. Strengthen your psychological fitness by building your self-awareness and self-belief. Learn to let go of petty resentments and needless negativity; practise self-acceptance and commit to the joy of lifelong learning.

There is so much in life you can't control. While you can't change what other people think, or do or say, you can control your attitude and how you choose to respond in any given situation. And expanding your happiness and well-being is a conscious choice, determined by the thoughts you choose to focus on, the emotions you choose to feel and by the actions and behaviours you choose each and every day.

Authenticity is golden in a world that is increasingly false, fragmented and fragile. Choosing to be really authentic means choosing affection and appreciation for others, creating abundance and cultivating an attitude of well-being. Inside every person is an inner child who wants to lighten up and live more in the moment. Wake up and become more aware of the poison dwarfs you experience in your life and the thoughts underlying them. Challenge the authenticity of these poison dwarfs. Are the thoughts underlying them genuine and true? Ask yourself: are you making assumptions, living in the past, comparing yourself to others, over-generalising or over-personalising any particular situation? Are you blaming or complaining? Have you distorted or dysfunctional thinking patterns?

The ability to reflect and learn from your experiences in life is a golden opportunity to grow, essential for your sustainable success and happiness. What's most important is not who you were, or even are right now, but who you are becoming along this journey called life.

So many people go through life making the same mistakes over and over again, often with increasing confidence! Struggling with the same weaknesses, never stopping to ask what they might do differently. Having the courage to regularly press the pause button and reflect allows you to learn something useful about yourself in a way that supports your making improvements. This can be a valuable way to gain meaningful insights into what is most important in your life, as well as to develop a better understanding of who you are becoming. Of course learning from your experiences also means appreciating and expressing gratitude for the many things that are going right, from relationships that work, to successes you have had.

Gardening the garden of your mind

Shut your eyes for a moment and imagine that your mind is a beautiful spring garden, filled with spectacular camellias, azaleas, magnolias and rhododendrons, a real spectacle of colour. These beautiful plants symbolise your happy dwarfs and you want them to flourish in the garden of your mind. However, your garden also has weeds which represent your poison dwarfs. You all know what happens to a garden that isn't weeded or cultivated: the weeds eventually take over and strangle the beautiful plants. Well, it's the same with your thinking. If you allow negative thoughts to fester, the poison dwarfs can take over.

Take complete ownership and appreciate that you are one hundred per cent responsible and accountable for improving your own emotional well-being. Ongoing effort is needed to garden your garden: to cut out the weeds and needless negativity from your life. Doing this will help you to cultivate the beautiful plants in the garden of your mind.

Bring on the brilliant and constructive thoughts that will produce the emotional positivity that will allow you to flourish in your personal life, professional relationships, and community engagements.

Don't forget to bring some of those happy dwarfs wherever you go, especially Enthusiasm and Fun. Increase the ratio of happy to poison dwarfs in your life (at least 3:1 and in your key relationships 5:1) so that you and they can flourish. Like any new habit, this can take some practice. Remember, the contagion effect of positive emotion can also help those around you feel even better themselves, which in turn will uplift you, creating a real win/win scenario.

Being committed to your happiness and well-being is about leadership and you can't lead others until you learn how to lead yourself. Each day, you have the opportunity to express the absolute best within you, to inspire by example, to influence each person you meet. Each day, you can choose to cultivate the happy dwarfs, no matter how loud the negative noise around you. Each day, you can strive to keep on improving and consider the ten commitments to expand your happiness. Express gratitude; be more kind and compassionate; nurture your relationships; work towards goals consistent with your values; make time for what matters; embrace exercise; cultivate realistic optimism; strive for simplicity; seek spirituality; choose happiness.

These ten commitments, to expand your happiness, will support your ability to work, rest and play at your best. I'm really optimistic about my goal that this book can make a real difference for you and mark a wonderful new beginning for your greatest assets, your health, happiness and well-being. Your happiness matters, it's really important and so worthwhile. Better again, expanding your happiness is *your* choice; it's within your grasp. You can choose, starting right now, to make these ten commitments a new benchmark for expanding your happiness, and the health and happiness of individuals, organisations and communities around the world. A living, breathing prescription opening up the possibility of enabling more happiness, for everyone, everywhere; spread the word!

The A to Z of happiness

- *Attitude* **of gratitude.**
- *Be* **more present.**
- *Courage* **to choose!**
- *Dare* **to dream.**
- *Exercise* – **the greatest pill of all.**
- *Face* **time with friends.**
- *Goals* **that allow you to grow!**
- *Hedonic adaptation* **(beware!)**
- *Integrity* **with your words.**
- *Journal* – **write it down!**
- *Kindness* – **give to live.**
- *Lighten up* – **laugh more.**
- *Mindful* **Meditation.**
- *Nature* **and Nurture.**
- *Optimism* – **oxygen for opportunity.**
- *Purpose* **and meaning.**
- *Quality* **experiences matter.**

A PRESCRIPTION FOR HAPPINESS

- *Reap* **what you sow.**
- *Spirituality.*
- *Time* **for what matters.**
- *Use* **your strengths.**
- *Volunteer* – **get involved.**
- *Why?* – **know your why.**
- *X-factor* – **go the extra mile to help others.**
- *You* – **you are responsible!**
- *Zip-a-dee-doo-dah!*

Afterword:
Discovering What Really Matters

This book project started with a fundamental question, 'How can you expand your happiness?' So often in life, it is not the initial response but the questions that follow that provide the real answers. Rather than holding on to what you know, open up the possibility of embracing uncertainty and learning from what you don't know. And so in trying to answer this question of how to expand your happiness in a way that is useful for you, the reader, I have opened up a series of other questions. Fundamental among these is your sense of purpose, your unique ability to live a life of meaningful contribution. Use your journal to consider some of the following questions that I believe will allow you to get in touch with the most real and authentic version of you: questions that go to the very heart of what it means to be human and support you in creating a compelling narrative for your life.

Who are you?

Do you understand what makes you tick? How do you describe yourself in terms of the various roles in your life? How do you live when no one else is looking?

Where are you going in your life?

Clarify your dreams, values and aspirations. Know your goals. In the *Upanishad*, one of the crown jewels in the Indian

Vedic body of literature, there is the following expression that highlights the deep connection between your goals and your destiny:

'You are what your deep driving desire is; As your desire is, so is your will; As is your will, so is your deed; As is your deed, so is your destiny.' To figure out that which you most desire deep down, ask yourself these questions. What do you want from life? What do you really want? What do you really, really want? Listen to the emotions of your heart and the logical reasoning of your mind. Listen carefully to the answers that appear and write them down in your journal. As your thinking changes and evolves over time so too will your choices. Heightened awareness and more insightful choices will support you to make better decisions in terms of your long-term happiness and fulfilment.

How are you spending your time?

Is it in a manner that allows you to do those things that are most important and meaningful to you? Are your heart and mind telling you that you should be spending your time differently, doing different things? Become really clear about what needs to happen to make this the best year of your life.

How can you improve?

How can you enhance your physical health and well-being; the quality of your thinking; your relationships? So, bottom line, how can you raise your game?

What's the one thing you could do that would lead to significant and sustainable improvements in your level of happiness in your personal life, work/organisation and community engagements?

What are you afraid of?

What would you like to put your time and energy into if

you were not struggling with your feelings or avoiding your fears? The fears you don't face in life often become your limitations. Once you have the courage to confront and face your poison dwarf called Fear, through greater self-awareness, understanding and belief, you have the opportunity for transformational personal growth and development.

What are you grateful for?

Who is helping you in your life? Who do you love? Who loves you?

The 'lookback' or legacy questions

Do you understand the difference between knowledge and knowingness, information and wisdom, success and significance? The word success is often defined by fame, fortune, and symbols of how many 'toys' you have. While success in life can be great, real significance can be so much better. Significance means putting others first: your legacy defined by the number of people helped and lives impacted, rather than simply the size of a bank account. You get to choose whether your legacy is one of significance or something less. Legacy is about greater vision, enabling hope and accomplishment, enriching the world by supporting others. So how do you want to be remembered? At the end of the day, what's the point in being the most successful person in the graveyard? Instead why not make a contribution based on your own unique strengths and interests? Rather than looking at what's in it for you, you are outwardly asking how you can better support others.

One of the best ways to build an even more fulfilling and meaningful life is to press the pause button regularly, to reflect and consider the following questions: What do you want your life to stand for? What are you here for? What makes your life worth living? What sort of person do you want to become?

A PRESCRIPTION FOR HAPPINESS

What is truly important to you? What sort of relationships do you want to build? How much of your potential have you realised so far? How can you find more meaning in the ordinary day-to-day experiences of life? What are you doing to become more kind and compassionate and to build a better world? How can you contribute more of your time, talents and energy to your community? How can you serve others? How can you make a difference? How can you expand your happiness?

Once you know your *why*, the *how* gets easier. So why not choose to open your heart and your mind to new possibilities and become the best possible version of yourself? Why not choose to be more of a leader in your own life, reach your mountain tops and create an inspirational future of love, hope and heartfelt joy? And why not now? You have so much potential for greater happiness within you. Not just some transient pleasure but really sustainable happiness that you can cultivate and self-prescribe freely and liberally, each and every day, for the rest of your life. The best time to begin is today and small incremental positive changes, made regularly, can transform your life. It's your choice, it really is. Expanding your happiness is up to you!

A PRESCRIPTION FOR HAPPINESS

EXPANDING YOUR HAPPINESS

THE TEN COMMITMENTS

PSYCHOLOGICAL FITNESS

- DEVELOPMENT
- AWARENESS
- ACCEPTANCE
- BELIEFS
- JOURNAL

Gratitude · Kindness · Relationships · Realistic Optimism · Exercise · Time · Goals · Choice · Spirituality · Simplicity

Acknowledgements

It is with a genuine sense of heartfelt appreciation that I want to express my gratitude for all of life's experiences, good and not so good, that have brought me to where, and more importantly, to who I am today.

Achievement and success, adversity and so-called failure can all be wonderful teachers on this journey called life and I have learned that everything can teach you something, if you are willing to use your experiences as an opportunity to learn. To really know and understand this and to be willing to embrace uncertainty can be so freeing and liberating, giving you an insight into the rich possibilities that your life offers.

I am especially grateful to all my teachers, current and past, who have been such a rich source of learning for me. In particular inspirational leaders and philosophers like Socrates, Aristotle, Gandhi, and all the others who were so ahead of their time; thank you for your courage, humility and timeless truths of wisdom.

And all the pioneers of evidence-based positive psychology, especially Martin Seligman, who, by demonstrating the courage to think differently, have created a whole new paradigm for happiness and well-being.

All my patients whom it has been a privilege to serve over the past twenty years; their stories have inspired me, their challenges have challenged me to think differently about health … and some of them have been my greatest teachers.

My experiences as a GAA sports team doctor for the Waterford Hurlers which gave me insights into the power of collective effort and determination, the price of achievement and perceptions around success and so-called failure.

The wider community in Waterford, especially those who have encouraged and supported the ideals of the Waterford Health Park as a resource to support improvements in health and well-being.

My colleagues and team at Waterford Health Park who have been such a privilege to work with. Those people who took time to read earlier drafts and cared enough to give me feedback especially Brian, Grahame, Jim, Monica, Tom and Phil. Heather Fennimore and Wayne Ruga who have both given me such support and encouragement.

Lee Grace for the illustrations. Janet and all at Kazoo Independent Publishing Services.

Especially my wife Edel, and three great children Malcolm, Tony and Lydia, who better than anyone know the time, effort and commitment expended here, and who make life so worthwhile.

And finally to you the reader, for your interest in expanding your happiness. This is for you. Thank you!

Further Reading

Authentic Happiness: Using the New Positive Psychology to Realise Your Potential for Lasting Fulfilment – Martin Seligman

Bounce: The myth of talent and the power of practice – Matthew Syed

Connected: The Amazing Power of Social Networks and How They Shape Our Lives – Christakis and Fowler

Counterclockwise: Mindful Health and the Power of Possibility – Ellen Langer

Creative Visualisation: Use the Power of Your Imagination to Create What You Want in Your Life – Shakti Gawain

Emotional Intelligence – Daniel Goleman

Flourish, A New Understanding of Happiness and Well-being – Martin Seligman

Flow: The Psychology of Optimal Experience – Mihaly Csikszentmihalyi

Gratitude Works! – Robert A. Emmons

Happiness by Design: Finding Pleasure and Purpose in Everyday Life – Paul Dolan

Happy Money: The Science of Smarter Spending – Elizabeth Dunn and Michael Norton

How to Stop Worrying and Start Living – Dale Carnegie

A PRESCRIPTION FOR HAPPINESS

Loneliness: Human Nature and the Need for Social Connection – John T. Cacioppo

Man's Search for Meaning – Viktor Frankl

Meditations – Marcus Aurelius

Mindset: How You Can Fulfil Your Potential – Carol S. Dweck

Peace is Every Step – Thich Nhat Hanh

Philosophy for Life and Other Dangerous Situations – Jules Evans

Poor Richards Almanac: Benjamin Franklin 1734

Positivity – Barbara Fredrickson

Self-Efficacy, the Exercise of Control – Albert Bandura

Self-Reliance – Ralph Waldo Emerson

Spiritual Evolution – George Vaillant

Thanks! How Practicing Gratitude Can Make You Happier – Robert A. Emmons

The Art of Happiness – The Dalai Lama and Howard Cutler M.D.

The Bhagavadgita – S. Radhakrishnan

The Blue Bird – Maeterlinck

The Blue Zones – Dan Buettner

The Emotional Life of Your Brain – Davidson and Begley

The Essence of Chaos, Lorenz Washington University Press

The Happiness Advantage – Shaun Achor

The Happiness Project – Gretchen Rubin

The How of Happiness – Sonja Lyubomirsky

The Lucifer Effect: Understanding How Good People Turn Evil – Philip Zimbardo

The Marshmallow Test: Mastering Self-Control – Walter Mischel

The Men's Health Book, A Guide for the Irish Man – Dr Mark Rowe

The Nicomachean Ethics – Aristotle

The Overview Effect: Space Exploration and Human Evolution – Frank White

The 7 Habits of Highly Effective People – Stephen R. Covey

The Seven Principles for Making Marriage Work – John Gottman

The Seven Spiritual Laws of Success – Deepak Chopra

Thinking Fast and Slow – Daniel Kahneman

Reading Group

Book Club Guide

- Did reading this book encourage you to open your mind to the possibility of seeing 'happiness' differently? If so, in what ways do you now better understand happiness?

- How do you deal with the Seven Poison Dwarfs in your life? And the Seven Happy Dwarfs?

- How can you ensure you have the right balance of Happy to Poison dwarfs to enable you to be at your best and flourish?

- Has reading this book encouraged you to take action and use some of my ten commitments to expand any aspects of your 'happiness'? Which ones and why?

- This book is filled with quotations from philosophers. Which ones did you associate most closely with?

- Do you agree that meaningful change begins on the inside? Consider the potential benefits of keeping a journal.

- How do you plan to develop yourself over the next ten years? Will you consider setting and working towards some new meaningful goals for your happiness and well-being?

- Small daily improvements over time can lead to amazing results. Do you agree with this?

A PRESCRIPTION FOR HAPPINESS

- ☋ What's the one 'small' thing you could do, starting today, that could make a significant difference to:

    - your health?
    - your relationships?
    - your self-development?
    - your happiness?